WILDLIFE
OUT YOUR WINDOW

Fascinating facts about 100 animals commonly seen in the Northeastern U.S.

Brad Timm, Ph.D.

All rights reserved. No part of this book may be reproduced, copied, or transmitted in any form, including electronic storage or retrieval without permission of the author. You can contact the author at the following email address to inquire about reduced cost bulk orders of this book (minimum of 10 copies) and/or to schedule a remote or on-site presentation or program by the author related to this book:

brad.timm@northeastwildlifeteam.com

ISBN: 979-8-9904432-0-4

This book was self-published by the author.
1st Edition. April, 2024.

Printed locally by CopyCat Northampton:
www.copycatink.com

Table of Contents

Introduction 3

Birds 7

Waterbirds
Belted Kingfisher 8
Great Blue Heron 9
Great Egret 10
Common Loon 11
Double-Crested Cormorant 12
Canada Goose 13
Mute Swan 14
Wood Duck 15
Mallard 16
Common Merganser 17
Hooded Merganser 18

Gulls
Herring Gull 19
Ring-Billed Gull 20

Hawks, Eagles, Falcons, Owls
Turkey Vulture 21
Osprey 22
Bald Eagle 23
Red-Tailed Hawk 24
Cooper's Hawk 25
Peregrine Falcon 26
American Kestrel 27
Great Horned Owl 28
Barred Owl 29

Common Backyard Birds
Ruby-Throated Hummingbird 30
Downy Woodpecker 31
Northern Flicker 32
White-Breasted Nuthatch 33
Blue Jay 34
Northern Cardinal 35
American Robin 36
Baltimore Oriole 37
Eastern Bluebird 38
Mourning Dove 39
Gray Catbird 40
Northern Mockingbird 41
European Starling 42
Common Grackle 43
American Crow 44
Eastern Phoebe 45
Cedar Waxwing 46
Tufted Titmouse 47
Black-Capped Chickadee 48
American Goldfinch 49
House Finch 50
Song Sparrow 51
House Sparrow 52
Carolina Wren 53

Other Birds
Wild Turkey 54
Pileated Woodpecker 55
Brown-Headed Cowbird 56
Red-Winged Blackbird 57
Wood Thrush 58
Ovenbird 59
Eastern Kingbird 60
Tree Swallow 61
Rock Pigeon 62

Mammals 63

Large Mammals
American Black Bear 64
Moose 65

Table of Contents

White-Tailed Deer ... 66
Eastern Coyote ... 67
Bobcat ... 68
Red Fox ... 69
Gray Fox ... 70

Medium-Sized Mammals
Beaver ... 71
North American River Otter ... 72
North American Porcupine ... 73
Fisher ... 74
Long-Tailed Weasel ... 75
Woodchuck ... 76
Raccoon ... 77
Virginia Opossum ... 78
Striped Skunk ... 79
Eastern Cottontail ... 80

Smaller Mammals
Little Brown Bat ... 81
Eastern Gray Squirrel ... 82
American Red Squirrel ... 83
Southern Flying Squirrel ... 84
Eastern Chipmunk ... 85
Muskrat ... 86
Star-Nosed Mole ... 87
Meadow Vole ... 88

Amphibians ... 89

Frogs and Toads
Wood Frog ... 90
American Bullfrog ... 91
Spring Peeper ... 92
Gray Treefrog ... 93
American Toad ... 94
Eastern Spadefoot ... 95

Salamanders and Newts
Spotted Salamander ... 96
Eastern Red-Backed Salamander ... 97
Northern Two-Lined Salamander ... 98
Eastern Newt ... 99

Reptiles ... 100

Turtles
Eastern Box Turtle ... 101
Painted Turtle ... 102
Spotted Turtle ... 103
Snapping Turtle ... 104
Wood Turtle ... 105

Snakes
Common Gartersnake ... 106
Northern Ring-Necked Snake ... 107
Eastern Milksnake ... 108
Eastern Hognose Snake ... 109
Common Watersnake ... 110

Appendices
How You Can Help Wildlife ... 111
Wildlife-Related Activities ... 120
Glossary ... 122
References & Related Readings ... 126
Wildlife Species Checklists ... 128
All Northeast Wildlife Species ... 138
Photographic Credits ... 145
Index ... 155
Notes ... 158

Dedication

*To Lukas, Jaz, Zeben, and Leo. I love you guys so much!!
I hope that this book helps inspire others to enjoy,
to connect with, and to conserve the natural world for
your generation and for future generations to come.*

Acknowledgements

First and foremost I'd like to thank everyone who, currently and in the past, has worked to conserve wildlife and the habitats which they depend upon; it is due to the work and dedication of these individuals and organizations that we are able to enjoy the vast diversity of species and natural spaces that we currently have. On a more personal level, I like to send a huge thanks to family, friends, and current and former colleagues for their support and inspiration across the many years. Thanks goes out to the Department of Natural Resources Science at the University of Rhode Island and to the Department of Environmental Conservation at the University of Massachusetts Amherst for everything during my times there throughout my undergraduate and graduate studies and research. Additionally, a big thanks to "the Biolab" at Cape Cod National Seashore for all of the support and community I enjoyed there through the years of my Ph.D. research. I'd particularly like to thank mentors K. McGarigal, P. Paton, and B. Cook for everything; I have learned so much, both professionally and personally, from you which I am forever grateful for. With particular regards to this book, I'd like to first thank M. Howell for your love, support, and enthusiasm throughout this entire process; I can't express to you how much that has meant. I also want to send a big thanks out to the following individuals for reviews of previous versions of this book which were instrumental in getting this book to its final state and to the finish line:
B. Compton, B. DeLuca, K. Doyle, M. Faherty, N. Freidenfelds, M. Howell, J. Kubel, K. McKenney, D. Pritchard, B. Thelen, and D. Wattles.

PREFACE

Having grown up in the Northeast in a family that enjoyed fishing, I was fortunate to spend much of my childhood outdoors. Whether it was on adventures with my grandfather in search of hidden fishing spots in the woods, mucking around in saltmarshes with a net trying to see what cool new critters I could catch, or exploring small patches of woods around where we lived, the one common thread for me was the excitement of the unknown... What types of fish might be in that new fishing hole? What types of fish might I scoop up in my net in that saltmarsh creek that I was waist-deep in? What animals might I come across in that patch of woods that I was exploring?

Here I am, some 25+ years since beginning my professional career in Wildlife Biology and Conservation, and I still often times find myself with those same moments of excited childhood curiosity when I find out something new about an animal that I thought that I already knew "backwards and forwards"...a single chipmunk often stores more that a gallon worth of nuts and seeds to last it through the winter?! ...orioles picks insects off of spider webs to eat?!

It is this continual awe and amazement that I feel when learning something new about the wonderful diversity of wildlife that we have in the Northeast that inspired me to write this book; this is a feeling that I want to help others to be able to experience, and to feel the increased connection to the natural world that comes with that.

I hope that this book helps you experience that awe, excitement, and connection. I am excited for you for your wildlife journey ahead!

-- Brad Timm

INTRODUCTION

GOAL OF THIS BOOK

The primary goal of this book is to provide an easily accessible reference of fascinating facts about common wild animals in the northeastern United States. Wildlife Out Your Window was designed to be informal and easy to understand for all audiences, not just people with a science background or previous knowledge about wildlife. Additionally, most of the wildlife species included in this book were selected because they occur across the full range of the human development gradient ranging from rural, to suburban, to urban communities and they are found throughout the Northeast; thus, no matter where you live, this book will be very relevant to you.

The broader goal of Wildlife Out Your Window is to help people from all walks of life expand their awareness of, and grow their connection to, the wondrous wildlife around them. I hope that through this book, readers are inspired to care about these animals and the broader environment they call home.

GEOGRAPHIC EXTENT

The geographic scope of this book is the northeastern United States (also referred to as "the Northeast") which encompasses Connecticut, Rhode Island, Massachusetts, Vermont, New Hampshire, and Maine. This is somewhat arbitrary, however, as the grand majority of the species in the region are found well beyond the Northeast. For example, all 100 animals included in this book are also found in New York State (and most are much more widely distributed than that). So Wildlife Out Your Window is even relevant to folks who live in areas outside of the Northeast.

The geographic extent of this book does not include the marine areas within the boundaries of the States listed in the previous paragraph, as the majority of people living in the Northeast don't experience these areas of the region.

INTRODUCTION

ANIMALS INCLUDED

A total of 100 different animals are featured in this book, primarily those that are the most commonly encountered in the Northeast and that are found in even the most urbanized areas. So whether you live in a rural area, a developed city, or somewhere in-between, Wildlife Out Your Window is for you! Birds, mammals, amphibians, and reptiles make up the 100 creatures featured; insects and other invertebrates were not included mainly because they are so diverse (for example, there are over 1,000 species of butterflies and moths in the Northeast!), and could not be adequately covered by a book of this scope.

SPECIES ACCOUNTS LAYOUT

Each of the 100 animals featured in this book has a single page dedicated to them containing their names (both their common name and their Latin name) and the Northeast States where they are found, a photograph, and a list of bulleted points of interesting facts about them. Interesting facts span a range of topics including when and where you can encounter them, what they eat, interesting behaviors they exhibit, where and how many young they typically have, conservation topics associated with them, and more.

INTRODUCTION

APPENDICES INCLUDED

Several appendices are included towards the back of this book which include simple things you can do to help these amazing creatures, wildlife-related activities you can do with others and on your own as well, checklists you can use to keep track of the animals you see, and more. After learning more about these animals, these actions and activities will help you feel more connected to them and to be able to help them so that they will be here for generations to come.

A RELATED RESOURCE

If you enjoy this book, check out the Northeast Wildlife Team website that is referenced on the back cover of this book (which can be accessed at www.northeastwildlifeteam.com). This website builds on the content of this book and includes regular features including wildlife conservation issues in the Northeast, links to other websites and books where you can learn more about particular wildlife topics, information about smartphone apps that you can download to help identify and keep track of wildlife you encounter, and so much more! Use this book and the continuously updated information on the website, to feel so much more aware of, and connected to, all of the wonderful creatures that are all around us.

"This we know: the earth does not belong to man, man belongs to the earth. All things are connected like the blood that unites us all. Man did not weave the web of life, he is merely a strand in it. Whatever he does to the web, he does to himself." --- Chief Seattle

"Only if we understand, can we care. Only if we care, we will help. Only if we help, we shall be saved." --- Jane Goodall

"An understanding of the natural world is a source of not only great curiosity, but great fulfillment." --- David Attenborough

BIRDS

Among the four wildlife groups included in this book, birds have the greatest species diversity in the Northeast by far. More than 300 bird species are regularly found in the Northeast, including some that are present in year-round and others only during specific times of the year. There are also an ever-expanding number of additional species whose normal range does not include the Northeast, but that unexpectedly show up, sometimes thousands of miles from their normal range, sometimes from across an ocean(s).

The life histories of birds of the Northeast are extremely diverse. They live in different habitats and eat different foods. Some migrate seasonally traveling both short and long distances, and some stay put. They have different parenting roles, including how they build nests and raise their young. And that's just the start!

Fifty-five bird species are included in this book, representing the greatest number of species among all four wildlife groups in this book, and many are quite familiar to people living in the Northeast. Those species that are included cover a range of different types of birds, and for the purposes of this book were grouped into five broad types ("Waterbirds", "Gulls", "Hawks, Eagles, Falcons, and Owls", "Common Backyard Birds", and "Other Birds"); these aren't standardized scientific groups, per se, but seemed to be a logical grouping into a small number of types that seemed relatively intuitive.

You can observe many of these species wherever you live in the Northeast, even in the most heavily developed urban areas. And most are quite easy for anyone to be able to easily identify. Once you attune your eyes and ears to birds, you'll likely be amazed at their diversity.

Belted Kingfisher
Megaceryle alcyon   ALL NORTHEAST STATES

Where: Wetlands, especially open ones including ponds, lakes, freshwater marshes with extensive open water, salt marshes, and rivers.

When: Year-round

Tips: Listen for their loud, chattering call that they emit when flying over the water and along the shoreline.

- **Adult size:** ~13 in. long, ~20 in. wingspan, ~5 oz.
- Females *(in photo above)* have chestnut coloring on chest and belly area; males have no chestnut coloring.
- Nest is in a burrow they excavate into a bank; can extend to six feet deep and usually slopes upwards so water stays out.
- Excavate their nest cavity using a combination of their bill and their specialized feet each of which have two toes that are fused together which improves their digging ability.
- Diet is primarily small fish; also eat insects, amphibians and reptiles, shellfish, small mammals, and berries.
- Regurgitate undigestible parts of their prey (such as bones and scales) in a pellet, similar to what owls do.
- Parents teach young how to hunt by dropping prey, such as dead fish, into the water for the young to "hunt".
- Have a number of fishing-related adaptations including: 1) specialized eye anatomy that gives them very precise depth perception (to judge the depth of fish in the water), 2) oils in their eyes that enable them to better see color, and 3) a transparent membrane, like a second eyelid, that covers and protects their eyes when they dive into the water.

GREAT BLUE HERON
Ardea herodias   ALL NORTHEAST STATES

Where: Wetlands, feeding in shallow portions near the shore. Nests are often in treetops of standing dead trees in wetlands.

When: Year-round

Tips: Look for them flying in the morning and evening, in Spring and Summer, during flights between their roosting areas and their feeding areas.

- **Adult size:** ~46 in. long, ~72 in. wingspan, ~5 lbs.

- Most commonly construct their large nests towards the tops of trees that are near, or in, water. Often nest in large colonies, sometimes containing upwards of 100 adults.

- Have an elaborate courtship which includes the male and female "bill clapping" where they snap their bill tips together.

- Can swallow fish that are much wider than their neck. Sometimes choke to death trying to eat a fish that is too big.

- Regurgitate food to feed to their young.

- Have specialized eye anatomy that gives them good night vision, enabling them to hunt both day and night.

- Have specialized chest feathers that continuously grow which they fray into a powder and apply to the rest of their feathers to protect them from oils and contaminants.

- On hot days, can be seen standing with wings drooped and extended from their body and with their beaks open (similar to dogs "panting"); helps to disperse heat and cool them off.

- There is an all-white subspecies, called the "Great White Heron", that occurs in coastal areas in the southeastern U.S.

GREAT EGRET
Ardea alba　　　　　　　ALL NORTHEAST STATES

Where: Wetlands, especially coastal marshes in the Northeast.

When: Spring – Fall; some are found year-round in coastal southern portions of the Northeast, particularly during mild Winters.

Tips: Look for them feeding in salt marshes, especially in southern parts of the Northeast where they are more abundant.

- **Adult size:** ~39 in. long, ~51 in. wingspan, ~2 lbs.
- Nest in colonies, often with other egrets and herons.
- Sometimes larger nestlings will kill smaller sibling nestlings (termed "siblicide"), to reduce competition, especially when food is scarce.
- Feed by stealthily stalking prey in shallow areas of wetlands, and quickly striking prey with their long bills, including fish, amphibians, crayfish, and other prey items. Sometimes will hunt insects and small mammals in fields.
- Will steal food from smaller heron species.
- Exposed skin from their eye to the base of the bill, which is normally yellow, turns lime green during the mating period *(see photo above)*.
- Prior to the Migratory Bird Treaty Act of 1918, the U.S. population was dramatically reduced due to the popularity of their "plumes" (long, gaudy feathers that they have during the breeding season) for women's hats and clothing. Their populations have rebounded since then due to that law and others passed to protect migratory bird species.

Common Loon

Gavia immer ALL NORTHEAST STATES

Where: Lakes and reservoirs during breeding season; often found on saltwater along the coast in Winter.

When: Year-round

Tips: Listen for their distinctive calls on Summer nights on lakes where they breed. Look for them from shore in coastal areas in the Winter.

- **Adult size:** ~32 in. long, ~46 in. wingspan, ~9 lbs.
- Have only one or two chicks each year. Chicks can swim and dive within two days after hatching; often ride on their parents' back during their first week.
- Loon legs are located very far back on their bodies, an adaptation that maximizes their swimming/diving efficiency, but that makes them very clumsy walkers on land.
- Can dive as deep as 200 feet and can stay underwater for up to ~5 minutes during dives. Typically place their head underwater to look for food before diving.
- Other diving--related adaptions include: 1) have solid bones (unlike most birds) which makes them less buoyant, 2) flatten feathers quickly when diving which releases trapped air and also makes them more streamlined, and 3) reduce their heart rate when diving to conserve oxygen.
- Population size throughout the Northeast experienced substantial declines from 1800's – mid-1900's primarily from habitat loss, hunting, and human disturbance. Populations have been increasing over recent decades due to protection measures put in place to reduce human impacts on loons.
- Ingestion of lead fishing gear (such as weights) can lead to lead toxicity causing severe neurological issues and death.

DOUBLE-CRESTED CORMORANT

Nannopterum auritum   ALL NORTHEAST STATES

Where: Coastal areas; large lakes and reservoirs in interior portions of the Northeast.

When: Year-round in coastal southern portions of the Northeast; Spring – Fall elsewhere.

Tips: Look for them standing on an elevated perch (rock or a dock/pier piling) near and/or above water with their wings spread to dry them out.

- **Adult size:** ~32 in. long, ~52 in. wingspan, ~3.5 lbs.
- Named for a curly black crest of feathers extending behind each eye during the breeding season.
- Breed in large colonies which can exceed 2,500 individuals.
- Adults' eyes turn bright turquoise blue-green during the breeding season; eyes are black during the rest of the year.
- Typically hunt for fish in relatively shallow waters (often less than 25 feet deep); are fast underwater swimmers and use their webbed feet for propulsion when swimming.
- Have a very prominent downward curved tip (or "hook") to their upper bill which helps them to capture fish; they also use this hook to help them climb rocky surfaces.
- Sometimes will vomit fish at a predator to try to deter them.
- Often seen standing with their wings spread to dry them out; need to do this as they have a lesser ability to produce waterproofing oil compared to many other waterbirds.
- Have nostrils, which is very rare in birds; the external nostril openings are permanently closed by adulthood.

Canada Goose
Branta canadensis   All Northeast States

Where: Wetlands with open water. Often found feeding in fields, especially in Winter when ponds are frozen over.

When: Some Spring – Fall; others year-round *(see related bullet point below)*.

Tips: Look for them in open water during the daytime and flying in V-shaped flocks to and from water during the mornings and evenings, respectively.

- **Adult size:** ~25-45 in. long, ~43-60 in. wingspan, ~4-10 lbs.
- Form "pair bonds" and stay with same mate for life; if one dies, the remaining goose will attempt to pair with another.
- Pairs with young often join other pairs with young to raise them together in a group; these groups are called "crèches", which is a British term for "daycare".
- Young often stay with their parents until the next breeding season the following Spring.
- Some are "migratory" and fly south for the Winter, whereas others are "resident" and don't fly south. Resident populations are largely descendants of captive geese that were used by hunters as decoys, before this practice was outlawed in the early-1900s. These decoy geese had their wings clipped so that they couldn't fly away.
- Fly in flocks in a V-pattern that maximizes flying efficiency as the goose in front of them reduces wind resistance. When the lead goose of the V gets tired (s)he moves to the back.

MUTE SWAN
Cygnus olor   ALL NORTHEAST STATES

INTRODUCED SPECIES

Where: Almost any large waterbody; primarily freshwater, though often found in coastal wetlands.

When: Year-round

Tips: Easy to identify as they are often the largest bird on waterbodies by a wide margin.

- **Adult size:** ~50-60 in. long, ~82-94 in. wingspan, ~25 lbs.
- "Mute" in their name is from them often being quiet; though have a series of noises and whistles they sometimes make.
- Introduced to the U.S. from Europe during the mid-1800s through the early-1900s.
- Have significant negative impacts on native ecosystems and wildlife species due to eating large amounts of aquatic vegetation and being aggressive towards other waterfowl.
- Fierce defenders of their nest; use their large wings to attack intruders (including humans) who come near their nest.
- Do not always pair for life, contrary to popular belief; some even have multiple mates at a time.
- During the breeding season the black knob at base of bill is much larger in males compared to females.
- Young swans (called "cygnets") sometimes ride on the back of one of their parents on the water and even under their wings.
- Fast fliers given their size; can fly up to ~50 mph.

Wood Duck

Aix sponsa ALL NORTHEAST STATES

Where: Wide variety of freshwater wetlands; often favor wetlands with a lot of vegetation in the water that they can hide within.

When: Year-round in southern portions of the Northeast; Spring – Fall in northern portions of the region.

Tips: Look for them swimming along the shorelines underneath leafy overhangs and along woody vegetation within the wetland.

- **Adult size:** ~18 in. long, ~30 in. wingspan, ~1 lb.
- Nest in tree cavities (often old woodpecker nest holes), usually in trees close to the edge of, or hanging over, water.
- Sometimes "egg-dumping" occurs whereby a female lays her eggs in another female's nest for the other female to raise; this occurs in a number of cavity-nesting waterfowl species.
- The only North American duck species that often produces two sets of young ("broods") per year.
- Use their sharp claws on their webbed feet to perch in trees.
- Acorns are among their favorite foods; have an expandable esophagus which can hold upwards of 20 acorns at a time.
- Were at threat of extinction during the early-1900s, primarily due to habitat destruction and over-hunting; populations recovered considerably when their hunting was prohibited between 1918-1940.
- Artificial nest boxes, often placed in wetlands well above the water line, have been very effective in maintaining and increasing population sizes.

Mallard

Anas platyrhynchos   All Northeast States

Where: Almost any waterbody; mostly freshwater ones.

When: Year-round

Tips: Often found in ponds in parks, cemeteries, campuses, etc.

* Don't feed wild ducks; it can lead to malnutrition, disease spread as a result of overcrowding, behavioral changes, and other negative consequences.

- **Adult size:** ~23 in. long, ~35 in. wingspan, ~2.5 lbs.
- One of the most abundant duck species worldwide; there are an estimated ~10 million Mallards in North America and ~50 million worldwide currently.
- Pairs typically form in the Fall or Winter and remain together until the female begins incubating eggs in the Spring.
- Females tend to select males with the brightest yellow bill coloration, which is likely an indication of his fitness.
- Young Mallards produce sounds while still in the egg, which is believed to enable them to synchronize their hatching so that they all hatch at the same time.
- Females *(on left in photo)* tend to be much more vocal than males *(on right in photo)*, emitting the classic "quacking" sound that most people associate with ducks; males make sounds mostly when fighting with other males.
- Have played a role in regional declines of the American Black Duck (a closely-related species), due to Mallards hybridizing with them and also from competition between the two species for food and nesting resources.

Common Merganser

Mergus merganser   ALL NORTHEAST STATES

Where: Rivers and streams in Spring – Fall; predominantly unfrozen portions of lakes and reservoirs in Winter.

When: Year-round

Tips: Look for large flocks in the Winter on large lakes and reservoirs, particularly during the period when smaller waterbodies are frozen over.

- **Adult size:** ~25 in. long, ~34 in. wingspan, ~3.5 lbs.; the largest inland duck species in the U.S.

- Nest in tree cavities along rivers and streams; these cavities are either naturally occurring (such as where branches have snapped off from the trunk) or are ones hollowed out by woodpeckers in previous years.

- Sometimes "egg-dumping" occurs *(see discussion in Wood Duck, page 15)*.

- Young leave the nest within a day or two after hatching, and will often ride on the mother's back when she is on the water during their first couple/few weeks.

- Young are adept divers within a week after leaving the nest.

- Predominantly eat small fish, and have serrated bills which helps them catch fish. Are sometimes referred to as "sawbills", which is a reference to their serrated bills.

- Propel themselves underwater during dives entirely with their feet and can stay underwater for longer than a minute.

- Their predation on fish can positively impact some fish populations by reducing unhealthy overpopulation.

HOODED MERGANSER
Lophodytes cucullatus   ALL NORTHEAST STATES

Where: Breed in wooded swamps. Spend Fall – Winter in almost any moderate-sized and larger freshwater body with open water, and sheltered saltwater bays, coves, and marshes.

When: Year-round

Tips: Many move to nearshore coastal habitats *(as listed above)* in the Winter.

- **Adult size:** ~18 in. long, ~24 in. wingspan, ~1.5 lbs.

- Males raise and spread the crest at the back of their head during courtship displays *(as shown in the photo here)*.

- Most commonly nest in cavities in trees located very close to the water's edge and often within 15 feet from the ground.

- Sometimes "egg-dumping" occurs *(see discussion in Wood Duck, page 15)*.

- Similar to Common Mergansers *(page 17)*, have a serrated bill that helps them catch fish, which are among their primary food items along with aquatic insects and crustaceans.

- Have a transparent membrane (called a "nictitating membrane"), like an eyelid, that covers and protects their eyes when diving.

- Heavily hunted from the late-1800s to the early-1900s. Due in part to reduction in hunting pressure, their populations have continually increased over recent decades.

- Increases in Beaver populations in the Northeast have likely aided in these population increases of Hooded Mergansers over the past century as the extensive wetlands created by Beaver dams often create ideal nesting habitat for them.

Herring Gull

Larus argentatus ALL NORTHEAST STATES

Where: Nest in a wide range of habitats, often nearby water; large nesting colonies on rocky islands. Found year-round at almost any coastal beach or marina; inland at lakes and reservoirs as well as commonly in fast-food restaurant parking lots.

When: Year-round

Tips: At marinas, especially those with commercial fishing boats, and coastal beaches are the most reliable places to see them.

- **Adult size:** ~25 in. long, ~58 in. wingspan, ~2.5 lbs.
- Often stay with same mate for life, until one of them dies.
- Male loses weight during courtship as he is focused on feeding his mate.
- Chicks peck at the red-spot on the parents' bill to stimulate the parents to regurgitate food for the young; this also occurs in other gull species (such as the Great Black-Backed Gull) where adults have a similar red-spot on their bill.
- Don't attain their adult plumage until they are four years old; until that time they are mottled brown-and-white.
- Able to drink seawater due to a gland they have, located above their eyes, that enables them to excrete salt from the water. Sometimes this salt can be seen being excreted from their nostrils and/or out from the end of their bills.
- Have declined in the region over recent decades, likely predominantly due to the decline of commercial fishing and the capping of landfills during this time frame.

RING-BILLED GULL

Larus delawarensis ALL NORTHEAST STATES

Where: Nest on the ground, often near freshwater. Found year-round at almost any coastal beach or marina; inland near/on freshwater wetlands as well as commonly in fast-food restaurant parking lots.

When: Year-round

Tips: One of the most commonly seen gulls inland.

- **Adult size:** ~17-21 in. long, ~48 in. wingspan, ~0.75-1 lbs.
- Named for the black color band around their bill.
- Attain adult plumage at 3 years of age; until then are largely mottled brown-and-white.
- Almost pushed to extinction due to collection of eggs and their feathers; since the passage of the Migratory Bird Treaty Act of 1918 their populations have not only recovered, but have expanded, as has their geographic range.
- Often steal food from other birds.
- Sometimes drop food in midair and catch it before it hits the ground. Unclear exactly why they do this, but thought that this is for play and/or for improving their hunting ability.
- Many migrate south for Winter; mostly migrate in daytime, in contrast to songbirds, which mostly migrate at night.
- Commonly return to same nesting site each year to breed and often their nest location is within ~10 feet of the location from the previous year.
- Have somewhat elaborate courtship behaviors which include a range of vocalizations and body gestures between the pair and numerous instances of the male feeding the female.

TURKEY VULTURE
Cathartes aura   ALL NORTHEAST STATES

Where: Found almost anywhere, especially in southern and central portions of the Northeast. Encountered more so nearby and above roads (searching for road-killed animals) and locations with expansive fields and open areas.

When: Spring – Fall. A small number overwinter in southern portions of the Northeast.

Tips: Look for them gliding in the sky in their distinctive V-shape.

- **Adult size:** ~26 in. long, ~67 in. wingspan, ~4 lbs.
- Skilled gliders, travelling on "thermals" (warm air rising from the ground) for long distances while rarely flapping wings.
- Fly relatively low to the ground, compared to many other "raptors" (hawks, eagles, falcons, owls, vultures, etc.), to detect the smell of dead animals.
- Have a very keen sense of smell that enables them to find food from far distances away; at times greater than one mile.
- Feed almost entirely on dead animals, often roadkill in heavily developed/roaded areas and dead livestock in agricultural areas. Sometimes will feed on rotting fruits and vegetables and are attracted to large compost piles.
- Frequently urinate on their legs which helps prevent bacteria from growing on their legs after standing on carcasses.
- Roost together at night in large numbers, which may include hundreds of individuals, and sometimes mixed-in with Black Vultures, a much less common species in the Northeast.

OSPREY
Pandion haliaetus   ALL NORTHEAST STATES

Where: Near large waterbodies including lakes, reservoirs, large rivers, and almost any coastal wetland.

When: Spring – Fall

Tips: Look for their large nests in salt marshes on human-constructed platforms. Also listen for their loud, high-pitched "chirping" call while they are soaring.

- **Adult size:** ~23 in. long, ~63 in. wingspan, 3.5 lbs.
- Fish often comprise greater than 90% of their diet.
- Dive after fish and grab them with their talons; they rotate captured fish to be facing head-first when they fly away with it, because that is the most aerodynamic position.
- Have a number of fishing-related adaptations including: 1) nostrils that can be closed during dives, 2) an oily waterproof coating on their feathers, 3) long and sharp talons, 4) an outer toe that can be angled backwards, and 5) barbed foot pads; the latter three being adaptations to better grab and to hold on to fish.
- Populations crashed between the 1950s – 1970s due to the widespread use of pesticides, and the pesticide DDT in particular, which caused their eggshells to become very thin and frail. Their populations have been continually recovering following the 1972 ban on the use of DDT in the U.S.
- Use a wide variety of materials to build their nest from. Can get tangled in discarded fishing line when collecting materials and while at their nest; has killed many individuals.

BALD EAGLE

Haliaeetus leucocephalus   ALL NORTHEAST STATES

Where: Forested areas near large waterbodies, particularly large lakes, reservoirs, large rivers, and coastal areas.

When: Year-round

Tips: The Connecticut River is one of the most reliable places to see them in the Northeast. There are Winter Bald Eagle "cruises" along the CT River in southern CT where you can go out on a boat to see and learn about them.

- **Adult size:** ~32 in. long, ~80 in. wingspan, ~9.5 lbs.
- One of two eagle species (Golden Eagle is the other) regularly inhabiting in the lower 48 U.S. States.
- Commonly breed with the same mate their entire adult life, until one of them dies. Often don't migrate with their mate, but re-form their bond when they return to the nesting area.
- Construct massive nests, made primarily of sticks and branches, that are typically ~4-5 feet wide x ~3-4 feet tall; the largest recorded nest weighed ~2 tons.
- Do not get their white head and tail until 4-5 years of age. At about 2.5 years old their brown head and tail start a slow gradual transition to white.
- Often steal food from other raptors, especially Ospreys.
- By the mid-1900s had become quite rare and were at threat of extinction, largely due to the pesticide DDT *(see discussion in Osprey, page 22)*. Have made a substantial recovery since the banning of DDT in 1972. In 1963 there were ~400 Bald Eagle pairs in the lower 48 U.S. States whereas in 2020 there were ~71,000 pairs.

Red-Tailed Hawk
Buteo jamaicensis   ALL NORTHEAST STATES

Where: Most frequently found along forested edges of fields and meadows, where they perch in trees to get a good viewscape of potential prey within the fields.

When: Year-round

Tips: Look for them soaring in the sky, especially when you hear their distinctive "keeeer" call. Also, are easy to see perched in treetops along highways during leaf-off times of year.

- **Adult size:** ~19 in. long, ~48 in. wingspan, ~2.5 lbs.
- Have intricate courtship displays which include the pair soaring in circles at high elevation and a number of steep dives and rises by the male. Sometimes will lock talons together and plummet in a downwards spiral for a time.
- Often mate with the same individual for their entire life.
- Both the male and female will incubate the eggs; the male will often spend less time incubating than the female as he will spend more time hunting to provide food for the pair.
- Will steal food from smaller hawk species.
- Often seen being chased by many smaller birds which is a behavior termed "mobbing". This "mobbing" behavior serves to help protect birds (including adults, young and eggs) in the area by chasing the hawk away.
- Distinctive "keeeer" call they emit when soaring is the sound commonly used in movies when showing a hawk or eagle.
- 14 subspecies of Red-Tailed Hawk throughout their range.

Cooper's Hawk

Accipiter cooperii　　　　ALL NORTHEAST STATES

Where: Forests, woodlands and suburbs; particularly near edges between woodlands and open areas.

When: Year-round

Tips: Look for them near bird feeders, waiting to ambush birds. Also, listen for their loud, repetitive "kek, kek, kek, kek" call during the breeding season as a good way to identify their presence.

- **Adult size:** ~16 in. long, ~31 in. wingspan, ~1 lb.; about the same size as an American Crow.

- Often use an ambush-style attack for hunting birds (which comprise the grand majority of their diet); stealthily perch on tree branches and then quickly launch after birds while deftly maneuvering through vegetation in the chase.

- Have short, rounded wings which is an anatomical design that enables them to be very fast and maneuverable fliers.

- Kill their prey most often by squeezing them to death with their feet; sometimes will drown their prey.

- Often pairs will mate for life; typically are only together during the nesting season and are apart the rest of the year.

- Males are ~2/3rds the weight of females, and females are very dominant over the males. Males are known to be quite cautious/wary around his female mate, likely because they eat other birds which are similar in size to the males.

- Eyes are yellow in year one, orange in year two, and bright red as adults (i.e., year three and beyond).

PEREGRINE FALCON
Falco peregrinus   ALL NORTHEAST STATES

Where: Nest on high locations such as cliff faces, tall trees, tall buildings and on tops of bridges.

When: Year-round

Tips: Look for them perched atop tall buildings in cities and also tall bridges. Often, seeing a flock of Rock Pigeons flying erratically in an effort to avoid predation by a Peregrine Falcon, is a good way to identify their presence.

- **Adult size:** ~16 in. long, ~41 in. wingspan, ~1.5 lbs.
- Often remain with the same mate for many years and will nest year-after-year at the same nest location.
- Mainly eat birds, often by diving at them from above at a high speed (up to ~200 mph) and capturing them with their talons. Sometimes just the force of the impact will kill the prey bird immediately.
- Have extremely powerful vision, which allows them to see prey from long distances away.
- Once the young have become skilled fliers, the parents will drop dead prey to them in mid-air to train them to hunt.
- By the mid-1900s they had become quite rare and were at threat of extinction, largely due to the pesticide DDT *(see discussion in Osprey, page 22)*. Since the banning of DDT in 1972, Peregrine Falcons have made a substantial recovery.
- "Peregrine" means "wanderer"; is a reference to their broad yearly range which sometimes spans multiple continents.

American Kestrel

Falco sparverius   ALL NORTHEAST STATES

Where: Areas with extensive open landscapes, such as fields, meadows, shrublands, and orchards.

When: Year-round (though in much reduced numbers during Winter). Absent in much of Maine during Winter.

Tips: Look for them perched on powerlines adjacent to, or within, open fields and meadows.

- **Adult size:** ~9 in. long, ~22 in. wingspan, ~4 oz. The smallest falcon in the U.S.; for comparison, they weigh ~1/8th the weight of a Peregrine Falcon.

- Males and females look quite different, which is rare among birds of prey. Notably, the male *(photo above)* has blueish-gray wing feathers and the females' are reddish-brown.

- Often nest in tree cavities, rock crevices, and sometimes atop buildings and utility poles.

- Have two black dots on back of head that mimic eyes; are used to confuse predators trying to sneak up behind them.

- In Summer they primarily feed on insects such as crickets, grasshoppers, beetles, butterflies, and moths.

- Because they can see UV light, they are able to track urine trails left by some rodents when hunting them.

- Have declined considerably in the region over recent decades, which is believed to be, in part, due to increases in Cooper's Hawks *(page 25)* in the region, which are predators of American Kestrels and of a range of other birds.

- Readily nest in nest boxes, which has been a successful conservation method throughout their range.

GREAT HORNED OWL
Bubo virginianus   ALL NORTHEAST STATES

Where: Forests and woodlands, particularly those nearby and/or containing open habitats such as fields, meadows, and yards. Also suburban areas, orchards, and swamps.

When: Year-round

Tips: Listen for their call at night, which sounds like "Who's a-wake? Me too.", especially during their courtship period which is from ~ Dec. – Feb.

- **Adult size:** ~22 in. long, ~44 in. wingspan, ~3 lbs.; the 2nd-heaviest owl in the U.S. (the Snowy Owl is the heaviest).

- The tufts of feathers atop their heads are not horns (are called "plumicorns"), and are thought to help them to camouflage and are also used in territorial displays.

- Eat a wide range of prey with rabbits, squirrels and other rodents being their most preferred; also eat amphibians, reptiles, and a variety of birds including other owl species.

- Primarily use vision for finding prey, which is aided by their very large eyes that are anatomically designed with many retinal rods for very good nighttime vision.

- Because their eyes are so large, they can't move them side-to-side like we can; need to turn their head to be able to see peripherally. Can rotate head as much as 270-degrees.

- Male and female call back-and-forth to each other during their courtship in the Winter; you can identify the male as he has a notably deeper-pitched call than the female.

- Do not migrate; pairs retain same territory year-after-year.

BARRED OWL
Strix varia   ALL NORTHEAST STATES

Where: Areas of extensive mature forest, and often those with wooded wetlands embedded within them.

When: Year-round

Tips: Listen, while you are in forests, for their very recognizable call which sounds like: "Who cooks for you? Who cooks for you all?" as evidence of their presence.

- **Adult size:** ~21 in. long, ~42 in. wingspan, ~1.5 lbs.
- Standing dead trees ("snags") and dying trees are very important for nesting and roosting. In addition to nesting in tree cavities, will also nest in former hawk and squirrel nests.
- Rodents typically make up most of their diet; sometimes amphibians can comprise upwards of ¼ of their diet. In some locations will hunt crayfish and crabs.
- Though they are one of the larger U.S. owl species, one of their major predators are Great Horned Owls.
- Have dark eyes, which is somewhat rare among owls; often found in owls that hunt at night, which Barred Owls do.
- Do not migrate; stay in same general area year-round.
- Increasing in the Northeast over recent decades as forests regrow and mature.
- Famous abolitionist Harriet Tubman imitated different calls of Barred Owls as a way to stealthily communicate with, and to guide, enslaved people at night during their escapes.

Ruby-Throated Hummingbird

Archilochus colubris   All Northeast States

Where: Areas where deciduous woodlands abut fields, meadows, yards, and other such open landscapes containing nectar-producing flowers.

When: Spring – Fall

Tips: Look for them visiting hanging flower baskets, flower gardens, and hummingbird feeders during the Summer; they particularly prefer red flowers.

- **Adult size:** ~4 in. long, ~4.5 in. wingspan, ~0.12 oz. (3.4 grams); for comparison, a penny weighs 2.5 grams.

- "Hummingbirds" are so named for the humming-like sound that is produced from beating their wings so fast.

- Ruby-Throated Hummingbirds beat their wings on average ~50 times per second, and as fast as ~200 times per second during some courtship displays.

- Can fly forward, backward, upside-down, and hover.

- At an average of only ~940 feathers, they have among the fewest number of feathers of any bird species in the world.

- Female constructs a small nest (~2 inches across x 1 inch deep); roughly the size of a large thimble. Nest may be held together, in part, by spider silk, which enables the nest to stretch as the young grow.

- Female lays 1-3 eggs; each egg weighs 1/50th of an ounce and each is approximately the size of a blueberry.

- Predominantly feed on nectar of flowers, insects and spiders, and sometimes tree sap.

DOWNY WOODPECKER

Picoides pubescens   ALL NORTHEAST STATES

Where: Woodlands (particularly deciduous woodlands and especially near the woodland edges), yards, parks, and orchards.

When: Year-round

Tips: The most common woodpecker seen in yards and parks throughout the Northeast.

- **Adult size:** ~7 in. long, ~12 in. wingspan, ~1 oz.; the smallest native woodpecker species in the U.S.

- Adult males *(depicted in the photo here)* have a red patch on the back of their head whereas females do not.

- Nest in tree cavities. The male and female excavate the cavity together which often takes ~1-3 weeks.

- Both parents incubate eggs; both will incubate during the day and the male does much of the nighttime incubation.

- Males and females often find food in different microhabitats during Winter; males often search for food on small branches (and even on the stems of weeds), females often search for food on larger branches and tree trunks.

- Sometimes will watch White-Breasted Nuthatches *(page 33)* and will steal their cached (hidden) food.

- Have specialized feathers around their nostrils that keep them from breathing in sawdust/wood-chips when drilling.

- Like many other woodpecker species they have stiff tail feathers which help brace them against the tree trunk.

Northern Flicker

Colaptes auratus   ALL NORTHEAST STATES

Where: Woodlands, yards, and parks; particularly areas with a lot of open area at ground level (to feed on ants).

When: Year-round

Tips: Listen for their loud, distinctive call which is often likened to a long, sustained laugh.

- **Adult size:** ~12 in. long, ~20 in. wingspan, ~4.5 oz.
- Underside of their wings and tail are yellow in the eastern U.S. and red in the western U.S.
- Males, in the eastern variety, have a prominent black patch (called a "mustache") extending back along their cheeks from the base of their bill *(see photo above)*. Females don't have this patch, and this is red in western variety males.
- Rival males use a "dance" to impress a female; the males face each other, sway their heads back-and-forth, joust with their bills, and flash (or "flick"; hence their name) their colorful underwing feathers. One eventually concedes and flies away.
- Can be seen standing on the ground covered in ants and rubbing them over their body; is called "anting" and has been documented in >200 bird species worldwide. Done to use the formic acid in ants to remove parasites and/or to soothe their skin after feather replacement.
- Primarily eat ants, in addition to a wide variety of other invertebrates as well as berries, nuts, and seeds.
- Eat ants by digging in the dirt, and have a long (~2 inches) tongue with sticky saliva that they lick ants up with.

WHITE-BREASTED NUTHATCH

Sitta carolinensis   ALL NORTHEAST STATES

Where: Mature woodlands (primarily deciduous woodlands), woodland edges, yards, and parks.

When: Year-round

Tips: Listen for their distinctive, nasally-sounding call.

- **Adult size:** ~6 in. long, ~11 in. wingspan, ~0.75 oz.
- Do not migrate and often stay with their mate year-round; may stay together until one of the pair dies.
- Female and male stay in very close proximity to each other.
- Have an interesting behavior known as "bill sweeping" where they rub the entrance to their nest (often a cavity in a tree) with mud, fur, plants, and/or crushed insects; this is thought to cover up their scent from being detected by predators.
- Like many songbird species, in the Summer they shift their diet to be almost entirely insect-based; during the rest of the year their diet is largely comprised of seeds and nuts.
- The name "nuthatch" comes from the phrase "nut-hack", which refers to their behavior of wedging their food (be it a nut, seed, or insect) into the grooves of tree bark and "hacking" away at it with their bills to open it.
- Sometimes "cache" (hide by storing) food, such as seeds from bird feeders, inside tree bark grooves to eat later.
- Are often seen walking head-first down trees.

BLUE JAY

Cyanocitta cristata   ALL NORTHEAST STATES

Where: Wide range of landscape settings, from interior forests, to woodlands and forest edges, yards, and parks. Particularly drawn to areas where there are oak trees (due to their preference for feeding on acorns).

When: Year-round

Tips: Very conspicuous where they are present due to their large size, bright coloration, and their propensity for being very vocal.

- **Adult size:** ~11 in. long, ~16 in. wingspan, ~3 oz.

- In the same Family ("Corvidae") as Crows and Ravens.

- Males and females look identical to us, but can tell each other apart from differences only visible in the UV spectrum.

- Their feathers are actually brown, not blue; they appear blue due to the way light scatters through their feathers, similar to the effect of light through a prism. Next time you find a Blue Jay feather, look at it when you light it from behind (for example, hold it up to the sun) and you'll see it is brown.

- Frequently "cache" (hide by storing) their food to come back to eat later. One radio-tracking study found each individual caching 3,000-5,000 acorns each during a single Autumn.

- Are excellent mimics and can mimic songs of a number of bird species. Often mimic hawk calls, which scares away other birds at feeders for a short time, giving them sole access to the food/seed.

- Use body language to communicate; the higher the crest atop their head, the more aggressive of a mood they are in.

Northern Cardinal

Cardinalis cardinalis   ALL NORTHEAST STATES

Where: Open woodlands, shrubby areas, yards, and parks.

When: Year-round

Tips: Listen for their distinctive loud call that sounds like "wheat, wheat, wheat, tew, tew, tew, tew".

- **Adult size:** ~9 in. long, ~12 in. wingspan, ~1.5 oz.
- Historic range was limited largely to the southeastern U.S., however has expanded substantially northward; believed primarily to be the result of backyard bird-feeding and warming winters over recent decades.
- One of a small number of songbird species in the U.S. where the female sings (in addition to the male). Females sing most frequently while sitting on the nest; believed to be for communicating with the male when to bring food to the nest and when to stay away from the nest if a predator is nearby.
- One of the earliest nesting songbird species each year and, as a result, they often have two broods of young per year.
- Males and females often observed attacking their reflection in car mirrors, windshields, etc.; occurs mostly during the nesting season when focused on defending their territory.
- Get their bright red coloration mainly from their carotenoid-rich diet (particularly carotenoid-rich berries and fruits). Rarely, bright yellow Northern Cardinals occur, which is due to a genetic mutation.
- Currently the State Bird of 7 U.S. States.

American Robin

Turdus migratorius   ALL NORTHEAST STATES

Where: Wide range of settings including forests, woodlands and forest edges, shrublands, yards, and parks.

When: Year-round

Tips: Commonly seen on the ground in yards, grassy fields, and parks feeding on worms. Also seen in relatively large flocks flying overhead during the Winter.

- **Adult size:** ~10 in. long, ~17 in. wingspan, ~2.8 oz.
- While some individuals are migratory, a large number stay in the same area year-round; this can vary from year-to-year, often depending on food availability.
- In Winter they often flock together and roost together at night; some roosts in the Northeast have been estimated to contain more than 25,000 American Robins.
- During warmer months they focus on eating earthworms early in the day and more on fruits/berries later in the day.
- Find worms mainly by sight, looking for very fine movements in the soil and grass. Often tilt their head when searching which enables them to see better because their eyes are located on the side of their head.
- Because they eat earthworms, often from lawns, they are particularly affected by herbicides and pesticides.
- Sometimes individuals can be seen that are "buzzed/drunk" from eating fermented berries; this happens most often in late-Winter/early-Spring.

BALTIMORE ORIOLE

Icterus galbula   ALL NORTHEAST STATES

Where: Open deciduous woodlands, forest edges, and in deciduous trees located within open meadows and fields.

When: Spring – Summer

Tips: Listen for their crisp, clear songs in the upper canopy of deciduous trees; they are among the most eloquent songsters of all of the Northeast's bird species.

- **Adult size:** ~9 in. long, ~11.5 in. wingspan, ~1.2 oz.
- Males take a little more than one year to attain their bright orange coloration.
- Very rarely individuals with a lot of red coloration are seen; this is due to these individuals eating a lot of berries from Morrow's Honeysuckle, a non-native ornamental plant.
- Nest is built by the female and is a woven basket-like pouch that hangs from the ends of tree branches. In the process, the female intricately weaves thousands of stitches.
- Like to eat fresh fruit, particularly dark fruits; tend to select ripe fruits over fruits that have not yet ripened. Leaving out oranges cut in half or jellies (especially dark jellies like grape or raspberry) are good ways to attract them to your yard.
- Sometimes eat fruit using a method whereby they stab soft fruits with their closed beak and then open their beak and use their tongue to drink the juice.
- In addition to fruit, much of their diet also consists of caterpillars which they will pick from the caterpillars' nest and insects which they sometimes pick from spider webs.

Eastern Bluebird

Sialia sialis   All Northeast States

Where: Open woodlands, forest clearings, beaver wetlands, meadows, and orchards.

When: Year-round in southern portions of the Northeast, Spring – Fall in northern portions of the region.

Tips: Look for them during Summer in meadows and fields where nest boxes have been installed.

- **Adult size:** ~7 in. long, ~13 in. wingspan, ~1 oz.
- As with Blue Jays and a number of other bird species, their blue feathers aren't actually blue *(see discussion on page 34)*.
- Male attracts a female by flying to a potential nesting cavity with nesting material and displaying to the female by waving his wings to get her attention.
- Females often raise two broods each year. Young from the second brood often stay with parents through the Winter.
- Predominantly eat a variety of invertebrates during Spring and Summer and fruits/berries during Fall and Winter.
- Some migrate south for the Winter while others remain near their nesting area; whether or not they migrate depends upon food availability and weather conditions.
- From ~1950 to ~1980 populations declined considerably mainly due to habitat loss and competition with other species. In particular, often are outcompeted for food and nesting sites by two introduced species, the House Sparrow *(page 52)* and the European Starling *(page 42)*. Widespread installation of Bluebird nest boxes throughout their range has been effective in increasing their populations.

Mourning Dove

Zenaida macroura   All Northeast States

Where: Grasslands, meadows, yards, parks, and sparse/open woodlands.

When: Year-round

Tips: Listen for their distinctive, mournful cooing song, which is how they got their name. Also easy to identify in flight due to their long, pointed tail combined with their rapid wing beats which make a whistling sound in flight.

- **Adult size:** ~12 in. long, ~18 in. wingspan, ~4 oz.
- Drink by sucking water up; most bird species drink by filling their bill with water and letting it run down their throat.
- Often feed on the ground, storing seeds in a portion of their esophagus called the "crop"; then fly to a perch to safely digest the seeds. Have been recorded storing thousands of grass seeds at a time in their crop prior to digesting them.
- Ingest bits of sand and gravel to help digest seeds they eat.
- When a predator is near their nest they sometimes perform a "broken-wing display", whereby they flutter on the ground mimicking having a broken wing to lure the predator away.
- Both the male and the female provide the young a milk-like liquid from within their "crop" for their first 1-2 weeks. This "crop milk" contains a wealth of antioxidants and immune boosters for the growing young.
- One of the most populous birds in the U.S., even though more than 20 million are shot by hunters each year.

GRAY CATBIRD

Dumetella carolinensis   ALL NORTHEAST STATES

Where: Any areas with dense shrubs and/or thickets.

When: Mainly Spring – Fall; small numbers overwinter in southern portions of the Northeast.

Tips: Listen for their very chatty song, which includes distinctive "mew" notes *(read below)*, in areas with dense shrubs and/or thickets.

- **Adult size:** ~9 in. long, ~11 in. wingspan, ~1.3 oz.
- Named "catbird" for one of their common songs that includes a note that sounds similar to a cat's "meow".
- Parents help shade young by spreading their wings while sitting or standing on the edge of the nest to block the sun.
- By comparing it with the first egg she lays in the nest, the female is able to identify a Brown-Headed Cowbird egg *(see page 56)* in her nest and will remove it, sometimes first puncturing it with her bill.
- Very skilled mimics; can mimic the songs of other bird species, treefrogs, and a wide variety of other sounds.
- Have a unique syrinx ("voice box") that is functionally split in two, enabling them to produce two different sounds at the same time.
- Is in the Family "Mimidae" (as is the Northern Mockingbird) which is named due to the ability of birds in this Family to mimic songs of other birds and other sounds. Is in the Genus *"Dumetella"* which means "dense thicket", which is most often where you will find Gray Catbirds.

NORTHERN MOCKINGBIRD

Mimus polyglottos   ALL NORTHEAST STATES

Where: Open areas that contain some shrubs and/or thickets including fields, meadows, yards, parks, and orchards.

When: Year-round

Tips: Listen for them somewhat maniacally singing their very complex songs comprised of songs from a wide diversity of other bird species, while they are perched on the very top of roofs, trees, and shrubs.

- **Adult size:** ~10 in. long, ~14 in. wingspan, ~1.7 oz.
- Extremely talented mimics; this species has been recorded singing songs of hundreds of other bird species. Can also mimic car alarms, dogs barking, frog/toad calls, and more.
- Their ability to mimic is believed to be a way that females select males to mate with, favoring males that include the most complex variety of songs of different bird species.
- Their Latin name *"Mimus polyglottos"* means "many-tongued imitator"; from "mime" meaning "imitator", "poly" meaning "many", and "glottos" referring to "tongue".
- Both males and females sing, though males sing much more.
- Often sing into, and sometimes throughout, the night.
- Have very notable white wing patches, which they flash quickly to stir-up/startle insect prey; also flash these as part of territorial behaviors.
- Aggressive defenders of their territories and nests, even aggressively attempting to ward off large animals such as hawks, house cats, dogs, and sometimes even people.

European Starling

Sturnus vulgaris   ALL NORTHEAST STATES

Introduced Species

Where: Open settings including suburban yards and woodland edges, agricultural fields (such as corn and grain), and urban settings.

When: Year-round

Tips: Look for their large flocks in Fall and Winter, often comprised of at least hundreds of individuals, most often present nearby and in agricultural crops such as cornfields.

- **Adult size:** ~8-9 in. long, ~12-17 in. wingspan, ~2-3.5 oz.
- Introduced to the U.S. in 1890 when someone released 100 individuals in Central Park of New York City in an effort to have the U.S. contain all birds mentioned in William Shakespeare's works. Have spread widely since then; currently the U.S. population exceeds 200 million individuals.
- Nest in tree cavities; outcompete many native cavity-nesting bird species which has led to declines of Bluebirds, Wrens, and other cavity-nesting bird species.
- Female often has two broods of young per year; often mates with a different male for the 2nd brood. The initial male typically doesn't help with raising the 2nd brood of the year.
- Sometimes lay eggs in the nest of other European Starlings.
- Are able to skillfully mimic songs of other bird species.
- Large flocks do serious economic harm to agricultural crops.
- Tips of feathers are white when freshly molted in Fall; darken over subsequent months.

Common Grackle

Quiscalus quiscula   ALL NORTHEAST STATES

Where: Open settings including open woodlands, woodland edges, marshes, fields, meadows, and yards; are particularly attracted to agricultural fields such as corn and grain.

When: Year-round in southern portions of the Northeast; Spring – Fall in northern portions of the region.

Tips: Large flocks are common in and around cornfields, particularly late-Summer – Fall.

- **Adult size:** ~13 in. long, ~17 in. wingspan, ~4 oz.
- Able to open acorns by combining "sawing" (using a hard section of their beak) followed by crushing with their beaks.
- Large flocks do serious economic damage to corn crops in many areas.
- Aggressive towards some other bird species including stealing worms from American Robins, and eating other birds' eggs, nestlings, and sometimes even adult birds.
- Can be seen standing on the ground covered in ants and rubbing them over their body; a behavior termed "anting" *(see discussion in Northern Flicker, page 32).*
- Nest in colonies; often numbering ~10-25 pairs, sometimes upwards of 100 pairs.
- Often join with other blackbirds (such as Red-Winged Blackbirds, European Starlings, Brown-Headed Cowbirds, and more) in large flocks during Winter, which can number into the millions of individuals.

AMERICAN CROW
Corvus brachyrhynchos   ALL NORTHEAST STATES

Where: Almost any setting often with exception to the interior of dense forests.

When: Year-round

Tips: Listen for their distinctive and loud "caw" call; note that the Fish Crow, a species that looks essentially identical, has a very similar call though is more nasally-sounding.

- **Adult size:** ~17 in. long, ~39 in. wingspan, ~1 lb.
- Often the young from the previous year will stay with the parents and help them raise next year's young; sometimes young from several consecutive years will stay as a family group with their parents.
- Juveniles look just like adults except have blue eyes (whereas those of adults are dark brown), and have pink coloration inside their mouth which is not present in adults.
- One of a rare number of bird species observed making and using tools to perform a specific task(s); for example, they have been observed on a number of occasions using a piece of wood to probe for insects in small crevices.
- Able to imitate a wide variety of sounds including songs/call of other bird species, barking dogs, honking of car horns, and even attempts to imitate human speech.
- Regurgitate undigestible parts of their food in a pellet.
- Roost together at night in Winter in large groups which can number upwards of 100,000 individuals. Daily flights between feeding sites in the morning and back to roosting sites before sundown often exceeds 20 miles each way.

Eastern Phoebe

Sayornis phoebe   ALL NORTHEAST STATES

Where: In open wooded areas, parks and yards; often nearby streams and/or human habitations (particularly rural and suburban homes, as well as farms).

When: Spring – Fall

Tips: Where they nest they tend to be very active nearby feeding and regularly making their "fee-bee" call, which can make them quite easy to identify their presence by. Additionally, they have a notable behavior of bobbing their tail up and down when perched.

- **Adult size:** ~7 in. long, ~11 in. wingspan, ~0.7 oz.
- Named "phoebe" for their song, which sounds like "fee-bee".
- One of the earliest returning migratory songbirds each year.
- Often nest around houses (under eaves and overhangs); also under bridges and in barns. Nest often made from mud and a mix of grass, leaves, and moss.
- Will return back to the same nest in consecutive years, which is not a common behavior of most bird species.
- Occasionally will overwinter in the Northeast, unlike other "flycatcher" species in the region.
- Diet consists primarily of a wide variety of flying insects such as bees, wasps, flies, ants, and others, and also fruit.
- Often return to the same perch they quickly just launched from to catch a flying food item.
- Characteristic tail-bobbing is thought to be to communicate to a predator that the Phoebe has seen it (even if it hasn't), and thus that it is not worth the predator trying to catch it.

Cedar Waxwing
Bombycilla cedrorum   ALL NORTHEAST STATES

Where: Pretty much anywhere there is an abundant source of berries; particularly forest edges in addition to orchards, old farm fields converting to meadows/shrublands, and downtown areas and suburbs.

When: Year-round

Tips: Listen for their high-pitched call in the Winter, when they are typically in large flocks especially in and around cedar and spruce trees. Crabapple trees, when fruiting, are also great spots to find them.

- **Adult size:** ~7 in. long, ~12 in. wingspan, ~1 oz.
- Named "waxwing" due to the presence of waxy, red-colored secretions on the tips of some of their feathers in some individuals. This is from berries they eat and specifically from a particular carotenoid that gives red berries their color.
- Some have orange tail tips instead of yellow, which is due to these individuals eating a lot of berries from Morrow's Honeysuckle, an ornamental plant introduced in the late-1800s. Orange tail-tipped individuals began appearing in the 1960s in the northeastern U.S. and southeastern Canada, coinciding with when this plant became more widespread.
- Fruit makes up the majority of their diet year-round, including almost the entirety of their Winter diet. They also eat insects in the Spring and Summer and even flowers.
- Very agile feeders and can pluck berries while standing upright or upside-down on branches, even while in mid-air.
- Don't regurgitate the seeds of fruit they eat, unlike many other birds, and thus readily spread seeds in their droppings.

TUFTED TITMOUSE
Baeolophus bicolor   ALL NORTHEAST STATES

Where: Most commonly in woodlands, and secondarily so in orchards, yards, and parks.

When: Year-round

Tips: Listen for their loud, crisp, and distinctive *"peter, peter, peter"* song/call. A very common visitor to bird feeders.

- **Adult size:** ~6.5 in. long, ~10 in. wingspan, ~0.75 oz.
- Closely related to the Black-Capped Chickadee *(page 48)*.
- Most frequently nest in tree cavities and, since they can't excavate those themselves, rely on existing natural cavities or ones created by other bird species such as woodpeckers.
- Often line their nest with hair. Sometimes will get this hair by plucking it directly from live animals, including Woodchucks, Virginia Opossums, squirrels, and other species.
- Sometimes one of their offspring will stay with their parents until the next breeding season and will help raise the young.
- During the Fall and Winter they often "cache" (store by hiding) lots of seeds, which is often why you see individuals continually coming back to bird feeders to get more seeds.
- Typically hammer open seeds with their bill while the seed is held between their toes while they are perched on a branch.
- Similar to that of a number of other songbird species, their range has expanded substantially northward over recent decades, believed primarily to be the result of warming Winters and backyard bird-feeding.

BLACK-CAPPED CHICKADEE

Poecile atricapillus   ALL NORTHEAST STATES

Where: Forests and woodlands, shrubby areas, yards, and parks.

When: Year-round

Tips: One of the most common backyard birds; listen for their distinctive calls/songs that include either "chick-a-dee-dee-dee-dee" or "fee-bee".

- **Adult size:** ~5 in. long, ~8 in. wingspan, ~0.4 oz.
- Migrate short distances seasonally, but stay in the same general region year-round.
- Flock together during migration and during Winter; often other small songbird species join these flocks. Birders use the presence of chickadee flocks as a good way of finding other (sometimes rare) birds, especially during migration.
- Store food items in a wide variety of locations and can remember hundreds (sometimes thousands) of these to then return to find and eat later.
- Use a variety of vocalizations for different purposes. For example, the more "dee" notes in their "chick-a-dee" call indicates a greater level of potential threat from predators.
- When predators are near nests the male and/or female will use distraction displays (including spreading their tail feathers, and raising and lowering their wings) in an effort to lure the predator away from the nest.
- In Winter they sleep individually in small holes in trees, which are critical for them to stay warm in cold conditions.

American Goldfinch

Spinus tristis   ALL NORTHEAST STATES

Where: Most frequently found in areas with meadows containing wildflowers that are adjacent to woodland and/or shrubland patches. Also common in parks and yards.

When: Year-round

Tips: Very common at thistle seed bird feeders. Also, are easy to identify overhead in flight with their characteristic undulating flying pattern *(see discussion below)* combined with their distinctive "chip" note.

- **Adult size:** ~5 in. long, ~9 in. wingspan, ~0.5 oz.

- Female selects male mate based on his bright coloration and on flight routines that the male performs.

- Nest later in the Spring/Summer than most other songbirds, timing their nesting often beginning in late-June/early-July so that seeds from their favorite plants (such as thistle and milkweed) are available to feed to their young.

- Have an almost entirely vegetarian diet, which is somewhat rare among songbirds. This works as an effective indirect defense against brood parasitism from Brown-Headed Cowbirds *(page 56)*, as often a Brown-Headed Cowbird chick that is present in a goldfinch nest can't survive more than a few days due to this diet limited almost entirely to seeds.

- Due to their predominantly seed-centric diet, they play an important role in dispersing seeds of various plant species.

- Have undulating flying pattern distinctive of finches; they flap their wings a few/several times causing them to rise and then stop flapping briefly, which causes them to descend.

HOUSE FINCH

Haemorhous mexicanus   ALL NORTHEAST STATES

INTRODUCED SPECIES

Where: Typically near human habitations ranging from suburban to urban settings, as well as parks and downtown areas.

When: Year-round

Tips: Common at bird feeders, often in areas where there are shrubby thickets nearby.

- **Adult size:** ~6 in. long, ~10 in. wingspan, ~0.7 oz.
- Native to western U.S., SW Canada, and throughout Mexico.
- In the 1940s, pet shop owners released House Finches on Long Island to avoid being charged for illegally selling them; have spread throughout much of the eastern U.S. since then.
- Females select males with the reddest color, which they get from eating a carotenoid-rich diet; the richer their diet is in carotenoids, the darker the red they are.
- A breeding pair will often have multiple broods of young in a breeding season. Often, while an earlier brood of nestlings are getting ready to leave the nest, the male will take over all of the care for these nestlings while the female builds a new nest, lays eggs, and begins to incubate this new brood.
- In 1994, a large number of House Finches in the Washington D.C. area were observed with red, swollen, crusty eyes; was subsequently identified as conjunctivitis *("pink eye")*. This can get so bad as to render individuals functionally blind. This has since spread throughout their introduced range and to native western U.S. populations; also has spread to other songbirds.

Song Sparrow

Melospiza melodia   All Northeast States

Where: Almost any relatively open area where there is some shrub cover nearby.

When: Year-round

Tips: Listen for their distinctive song, which is typically three or four short notes followed by a variable trill. Often conspicuously perch on a tree, shrub, or on another object when singing, so can be relatively easy to see.

- **Adult size:** ~6 in. long, ~8 in. wingspan, ~0.7 oz.
- This is the classic backyard sparrow that is present year-round in suburban areas throughout the region.
- Are found, at some point during the year, in every U.S. State except for Hawaii.
- There are more than 30 Song Sparrow subspecies combined throughout the U.S., Canada, and Mexico; there is quite a bit of variability among these subspecies in their appearance.
- Males sing upwards of 20 variations of their song, often learning variants from males that live nearby. Females are attracted to the uniqueness of a given male's song variant in addition to those males whose song best resembles that of his parents.
- Sometimes, in very heavily lit urban areas, some will sing throughout the night. One theory of why they (and some other bird species) sing at night in urban areas is that noise pollution tends to be less at night, and thus their singing may be more effective (for example, for attracting mates or for defining their territory) during those times.

House Sparrow

Passer domesticus   All Northeast States

Introduced Species

Where: Typically near human habitations ranging from suburban to urban settings, farms, as well as parks and downtown areas.

When: Year-round

Tips: Readily encountered in urban and downtown areas while feeding in small flocks on the ground.

- **Adult size:** ~6-7 in. long, ~7.5-10 in. wingspan, ~1 oz.

- Introduced to various parts of the U.S. in mid-1850's; have spread widely since then. Are currently found throughout the lower 48 U.S. States and other portions of North America.

- Was introduced primarily to reduce worm and caterpillar populations in city parks that were causing tree defoliation.

- Nest in tree cavities and birdhouses; often evict other bird species already nesting in these locations.

- Nest earlier in the year than most songbirds; gives them an advantage in securing prime nesting locations.

- Can have up to four broods of young per year as a result of beginning nesting early in the year.

- Often take "dust baths" for feather maintenance; fine dirt particles absorb oils from feathers which they then shake off. Dust baths also help remove mites, lice, and dry skin.

- Males *(in photo above)* with more black on their throat tend to be dominant over males with less black on their throat.

- Often feed in small flocks as a "safety in numbers" strategy and so that they can keep a better watch for predators.

CAROLINA WREN

Thryothorus ludovicianus   ALL NORTHEAST STATES

Where: Typically open areas that have a good amount of shrubs and/or thickets nearby; frequently found in yards.

When: Year-round

Tips: Look for them often active on the ground and on, and around, wood piles and brush piles. Listen for their loud and distinctive "tea-kettle, tea-kettle, tea-kettle" song.

- **Adult size:** ~5.5 in. long, ~7.5 in. wingspan, ~0.75 oz.
- Expanded their range northward and into the Northeast during the latter half of the 1900s, which is thought to be largely due to warming Winters and backyard bird-feeding.
- Are not migratory and stay in the same area year-round.
- Male and female often pair up and mate together for life, or until one of the pair dies.
- The male, as in some other Wrens, often constructs more than one nest, from which the female will select just one. The purpose of constructing multiple nests isn't fully understood, but is thought to be some combination of: 1) a way for a female to better assess the male's nest-construction ability, 2) to provide extra nests for resting/roosting in, and 3) to use these extra nests to deceive predators.
- Spend much of their time on the ground searching for a variety of invertebrate prey while sifting through debris piles, firewood stacks, leaves, under tree bark, in vegetation, etc.
- Because they spend a lot of time on the ground, large numbers are killed by cats allowed to roam-free outdoors.

Wild Turkey
Melagrus gallopavo   All Northeast States

Where: Areas where forests and woodlands (particularly deciduous or deciduous-dominated ones) are interspersed with open areas such as fields and meadows.

When: Year-round

Tips: Look for them feeding in large flocks in fields adjacent to forests and woodlands.

- **Adult size:** Males: ~46 in. long, ~64 in. wingspan, ~16 lbs. Females: ~38 in. long, ~50 in. wingspan, ~9 lbs.
- Have extremely powerful vision which is ~3-times sharper than our 20/20 vision.
- Male will mate with multiple females, sometimes more than 10, in a breeding season. After breeding, males will join all male flocks and the females will lay their eggs and raise the young without help from the male. Females often will join with other females and their young to raise them together.
- Females sometimes lay eggs in nests of other Turkeys, and rarely in Ruffed Grouse nests, for them to raise their young.
- Are quite agile fliers; roost in trees at night for safety.
- Male Turkey droppings are J-shaped and those of females are spiral-shaped.
- Were at threat of extinction in the early-1900s with the U.S. population < 200,000 individuals.
- Extensive conservation efforts, including widespread re-introductions, have resulted in population increases throughout the Northeast in recent decades.

Pileated Woodpecker

Dryocopus pileatus   All Northeast States

Where: Mature forests and woodlands.

When: Year-round

Tips: Look for large rectangular holes dug out in trees by Pileated Woodpeckers as evidence of their presence. These are made when searching primarily for Carpenter Ants, which are among their most favored food items.

- **Adult size:** ~17 in. long, ~29 in. wingspan, ~10 oz.; the largest North American woodpecker (the Ivory-Billed Woodpecker was larger but is believed to be extinct).

- Named "Pileated" from the Latin word "pileatus" which means "capped"; refers to the bright red top of their head.

- Male and female both help excavate the nesting cavity. Rarely will re-use the nesting cavity in subsequent years, but these are often used in future years by other bird species or by a range of different cavity-nesting mammals, such as Raccoons and Flying Squirrels.

- Male and female of a given pair roost in a different cavity from each other at night.

- They don't migrate; pair remain together on their territory year-round.

- Males *(in photo above)* have a red cheek stripe on each cheek whereas the cheek stripe of females is entirely black.

- Have a very long tongue which is equipped with barbs and sticky saliva that they use to extract insects (especially ants) and insect larvae from within holes that they drill in trees.

Brown-Headed Cowbird

Molothrus ater   All Northeast States

Where: Wide range of open settings such as grasslands, fields, meadows, shrublands, and yards. Not often found in forests, but will be found in woodland edges nearby openings.

When: Spring – Fall

Tips: Listen for their distinctive song which sounds like a high-pitched gurgle followed by a short, very high-pitched whistle. Look for them within large flocks of a variety of blackbird species in cornfields in the Fall.

- **Adult size:** ~7.5 in. long, ~12 in. wingspan, ~1.5 oz.
- Up until the 1800s, the Great Plains comprised much of their range, when they often followed Bison herds. Spread widely since then due to widespread forest-clearing. Currently their range extends throughout the entirety of the lower 48 U.S. States (and northern Mexico and much of Canada).
- Lay their eggs in the nests of other bird species (> 200 species documented); this is known as "brood parasitism". Lay a single egg in each of a large number of different nests.
- Their egg tends to hatch faster than the host species' eggs, their chick exaggeratedly begs for food and is much larger than the host species' chicks; all are adaptations giving their chick a significant advantage over the host species' chicks.
- Some species have learned to identify the presence of a cowbird egg in their nest, and will either remove the egg or abandon the nest and re-nest at another location.
- As they don't have to spend time and energy raising their own chicks, a female can lay a large number of eggs (sometimes > 30) in a single breeding season.

Red-Winged Blackbird

Agelaius phoeniceus   ALL NORTHEAST STATES

Where: Freshwater and saltwater marshes, and grasslands/meadows.

When: Primarily Spring – Fall; a relatively small proportion of individuals overwinter in the Northeast.

Tips: Listen for their distinctive "konk-ra-leee" song in marshes and grasslands.

- **Adult size:** ~9 in. long, ~13 in. wingspan, ~1.8 oz.

- Male commonly has several females within his territory which he mates with; sometimes as many as 15 females.

- To defend their territory and to attract mates, males perch atop a high stalk of vegetation (commonly a cattail or reed grass ("*Phragmites*")) and sing with their feathers fluffed out, tail partially spread, and their wings slightly lifted to prominently display their bright red shoulder patches.

- Males will aggressively attack intruders (including other birds, mammals, and even humans) that enter their territory.

- Roost in large numbers at night and, in the Winter, flocks can number well in to the thousands of individuals.

- One of the most populous bird species in the U.S. with a current population > 100 million individuals; however, the population has declined by ~30% over the past 50 years.

- Arrival of Red-Winged Blackbirds from their wintering grounds is often considered an early "sign of Spring".

Wood Thrush

Hylocichla mustelina ALL NORTHEAST STATES

Where: Mature deciduous and mixed forests and woodlands.

When: Spring – Fall

Tips: Listen for their crisp, melodic song as evidence of their presence. Note that their song sounds somewhat similar to that of the Hermit Thrush, though is more crisp than that of the Hermit Thrush.

- **Adult size:** ~8 in. long, ~13 in. wingspan, ~1.5 oz.
- A talented singer with a beautiful, albeit somewhat mournful, song with a flute-like quality to it. Individual males can sing upwards of 50 variations of the species' song.
- ~50% of pairs have two broods in a year; male does most of the feeding of the young in their first brood so that the female can build a second nest to raise the second brood.
- The eggs of upwards of 25% of females in some areas will be fathered by a male other than the female's mate.
- Feed on the forest floor, searching through leaves for insects, as well as salamanders and snails. Snail shells are especially important for females to accumulate calcium for egg shell development; also eat a variety of berries.
- Have declined significantly throughout their range over the past ~50 years, largely the result of habitat loss, brood-parasitism by Brown-Headed Cowbirds *(page 56)*, and decline of invertebrate prey due to acid rain (especially snails, due to their importance for egg development).

OVENBIRD

Seiurus aurocapilla   ALL NORTHEAST STATES

Where: Mature deciduous and mixed forests.

When: Spring – Fall

Tips: Listen for their loud, distinctive, and repetitive two-note song which sounds like "tea-cher, tea-cher, tea-cher".

- **Adult size:** ~6 in. long, ~9.5 in. wingspan, ~0.7 oz.
- Named "Ovenbird" because their nest is shaped similar to a Dutch oven. Nest often is built on the forest floor or not far above the ground in shrubs; made from a combination of vegetation material and sometimes hair as well. Camouflage nest with leaves, branches, and other vegetation material.
- If a predator comes near the nest the female often tries to lure it away by pretending that she has a broken wing.
- Often Ovenbirds nearby each other will sing at the same time, though alternating so as not to overlap one another.
- Spend most of their time on the ground looking under leaves for invertebrates to eat; during Winter will also incorporate a good amount of seeds and fruits to their diet.
- Has long legs and walks on the ground and branches, rather than hop like most warblers do. Sometimes referred to as the "Walking Warbler".
- Require large tracts of contiguous forest for breeding and thus are negatively impacted by forest fragmentation.

Eastern Kingbird

Tyrannus tyrannus   All Northeast States

Where: Open areas such as meadows, shrublands, parks, and orchards; woodland edges, wetland edges, and marshes such as beaver ponds.

When: Spring – Fall

Tips: Look for them conspicuously perched atop branches, shrubs, wire fencing, etc.; listen for their repeated, high-pitched call and for their fluttering flight pattern when they are actively hunting from these perches.

- **Adult size:** ~8.5 in. long, ~15 in. wingspan, ~1.5 oz.
- Member of the Flycatcher Family; feed mainly on beetles, moths, bees, wasps, and dragonflies in Spring-Summer. Will also eat small frogs and small rodents, as well as some fruit.
- Regurgitate undigestible skeletal parts of prey.
- Remove stingers from bees/wasps before feeding to young.
- Aggressive towards other birds in their territory (including much larger species); often attack and chase them away.
- Both males and females have a reddish-orange patch on the top of their head, though this patch is very rarely seen by humans. Will raise their feathers atop their head during mating and defensive behaviors.
- The female is able to identify a Brown-Headed Cowbird egg *(see page 56)* in her nest and will remove it from the nest.
- Sometimes a female will lay her eggs in another female's nest in an attempt to have the other female raise her young.
- Switch their diet to be predominantly fruit-based while at their overwintering grounds in South America.

TREE SWALLOW

Tachycineta bicolor   ALL NORTHEAST STATES

Where: Wide variety of open areas such as fields, meadows, marshes, and beaver ponds; require existing tree cavities for nesting locations.

When: Spring – Fall

Tips: Look for massive flocks, often numbering well into the thousands of individuals, in late-Summer – early-Fall prior to their migration southward for the Winter.

- **Adult size:** ~6 in. long, ~14 in. wingspan, ~0.7 oz.
- Nests often built in tree cavities, often cavities previously created by woodpeckers. Will also readily nest in nest boxes.
- Females do all of the nest-building, incubation of the eggs, and rearing of the young; male helps feed the young.
- Flying insects make up the majority of their food items and will also pick off insects from the surface of water. They supplement this food with berries and seeds as well.
- Eat more berries than other swallow species, which enables them to stay on their breeding grounds longer and results in them not needing to migrate as far as other swallows.
- Bathe themselves by swooping down over water and gently make contact with the water and then shake their bodies to disperse the water as they fly upwards. Will also actively bathe themselves during rain events.
- During the non-breeding season tree swallows gather in flocks that often number into the thousands of individuals, sometimes exceeding 100,000 individuals.

ROCK PIGEON
Columba livia   ALL NORTHEAST STATES

INTRODUCED SPECIES

Where: Urban areas and farms with accessible barns.

When: Year-round

Tips: In urban areas for them in parks and perched and/or nesting along the sides of tall brick buildings. Also, are common under highway overpasses almost anywhere in the region.

- **Adult size:** ~13 in. long, ~28 in. wingspan, ~9 oz.
- Originally from Europe and was introduced into North America in the early-1600s. Since then have expanded throughout the entirety of the lower 48 U.S. States, into Alaska, and throughout much of southern Canada.
- Often remain with same mate for life, until one of them dies.
- Male incubates the eggs typically from mid-morning until late-afternoon; the female incubates the rest of the time.
- Both male and female provide the young a milk-like liquid from within their "crop" *(see discussion in Mourning Dove, page 39)*.
- Most common color variant is in the photo above; can vary considerably including some that are mostly white.
- Have an amazing ability to find their way home and use the Earth's magnetic field to navigate. Were often used to send messages historically, as recently as in World War II.
- Drink water by sucking it up, unlike most other birds *(see discussion in Mourning Dove, page 39)*.

Mammals

Among the four wildlife groups included in this book, mammals have the second-greatest species diversity in the region. A total of 78 mammal species live in the Northeast, which include 16 marine species (including seals, whales, and porpoises). All of the Northeast mammals are present year-round in the region except for the marine species and some of the bats. Many of the mammal species in the region slow down in the winter and spend less time on the surface when it is especially cold.

The life histories of Northeast mammals are quite diverse. They live in different habitats, have varied home range sizes and eat very different foods. Some are active any time of the day or night, some are mainly active during dawn and dusk, while others are only active at night

This book covers 25 of the 78 mammal species in the Northeast. This book doesn't cover the six marine species because these are not usually seen by most people in the region. The species the book covers are ones that are most familiar to the general public. The book also includes two less familiar but intriguing species, the Star-Nosed Mole and Gray Fox, which both have interesting life histories. The 25 mammal species were grouped into three broad types based on their body size, Large, Medium, and Small.

Most of these mammals are found throughout the Northeast and many are found even in the most heavily developed urban areas. Some, such as the Gray Squirrel and Eastern Cottontail, are very commonly seen as they tend to be fairly accustomed to humans. Others, however are more skittish around humans and thus are less frequently encountered by people, but if you know where and when to look for them, you can increase your chances of catching a glimpse of them too!

American Black Bear

Ursus americanus ALL NORTHEAST STATES

Where: Forested areas, especially those near wetlands. Also suburban areas where they eat bird seed from bird feeders and eat garbage.

Tips: Consider not putting out bird feeders if you have bears nearby, as these attract bears.

- **Adult size:** In the Northeast, males ("boars") are often ~200-450 lbs. (can exceed 600 lbs.) and females ("sows") ~150-200 lbs. (can be up to 300 lbs.). Adults are ~5-6 feet long.

- **Diet:** In Spring they feed on grasses and newly emerging succulent plants. In Summer they take advantage of more nutritious foods including ripening berries, fruits, and insects. In Fall they shift to nuts, acorns, and ripened corn.

- Live an average of ~20 years in the wild.

- In eastern U.S. fur (other than snout) is predominantly black; often have brown and/or blond color mixed-in iwestern U.S.

- They den from late-Fall until late-Winter/early-Spring. Dens often are under fallen trees, in brush piles, in large rock crevices, or in mountain laurel thickets.

- Female gives birth to a litter of typically 2-3 cubs sometime in mid-to-late January; each are less than 1 pound when born. The cubs remain with their mother for ~18 months.

- During denning their heart rate and metabolism drop by ~75% and they consume upwards of 25% of their body weight. In Winters with abundant food available, some may not den long.

- Are great climbers; climb trees to escape perceived threats, to protect their young, and to rest.

- Black Bear populations are continually increasing in the region and are believed to be at their highest levels since widespread European settlement throughout the Northeast 200+ years ago.

Moose
Alces alces   ALL NORTHEAST STATES

Where: Forested areas, especially those with wetlands and recent forest openings.

Tips: Be careful when driving in areas with high moose density, as moose-vehicle collisions have high human injury and fatality rates.

- **Adult size:** Males ("bulls") are often ~600-1,000+ lbs., females ("cows") ~500-750 lbs. Adults commonly reach 6 feet in height at their shoulders, with 3-4 foot-long legs, and are 8-10 feet long from their nose to the end of their body.

- **Diet:** Eat a wide range of plant material including soft, green vegetation in Summer, twigs, buds, bark, and conifer needles (esp. fir and hemlock) in Winter. Typically eat ~40-60 lbs. daily.

- Can live ~20 years but the average lifespan is ~10-12 years.

- Cows give birth to 1-2 calves in mid-Spring; calves are ~20-25 lbs. at birth and reach ~300-400 lbs. by Fall. Calves remain with their mother for ~1 year; she drives them away prior to her next birthing.

- Bulls begin growing antlers each year in March/April, which are fully grown by ~August, and are shed in December/January.

- Antlers, which may be 5 feet wide and up to 50 lbs., are used to display a bull's physical prowess during the mating season and are used in male-to-male combats for females.

- Populations throughout much of the Northeast have been drastically declining since the early-2000s primarily due to Winter Ticks. Winter Tick is a species that has been increasing in the region due to warming Winters caused by climate change. In some areas of the Northeast, upwards of 50% of calves die during their first Winter due to being infested with thousands of Winter Ticks; can lead to ~20%-30% weight loss.

WHITE-TAILED DEER
Odocoileus virginianus   ALL NORTHEAST STATES

Where: Areas where forest and fields/lawns abut each other. Particularly prefer areas of regenerating forest.

Tips: Make sure to wear blaze orange clothing when hiking during hunting seasons so you are clearly visible to hunters.

- **Adult size:** Males ("bucks") are often ~125-250 lbs. (can exceed 300 lbs.), females ("does") ~80-150 lbs. Adults are ~3-3.5 feet in height at their shoulders and are ~6 feet long. They tend to be larger the further north you are in the region.

- **Diet:** Primarily eat live plants in Spring and Summer; corn, acorns, and other nuts in the Fall; buds and twigs of woody plants in Winter.

- Males grow and shed their antlers each year.

- Can run 30+ mph, jump as high as 10 feet and as far as 30 feet.

- They can't see well in the red-to-orange spectrum; they see blaze orange (color of hunting vests and hats) as a dull brown.

- Deer overpopulation occurs in many areas of the Northeast due to extensive deer habitat (forests/woodlands abutting open, vegetated areas) created by suburban human development, combined with reduction of natural predators and reduced hunting in recent decades.

- Controlling deer populations, such as by hunting, is important because if deer populations get too large this can lead to over-browsing, causing: 1) a reduction of food for deer (and thus overall underfed and unhealthy deer), and 2) also severely limits forest regeneration (due to deer eating tree seedlings) which also leads to a reduction in overall forest biodiversity.

Eastern Coyote
Canis latrans   All Northeast States

Where: Almost any landscape setting as long as there is some wooded area.

Tips: Listen for them vocalizing at night in areas where fields and woodlands abut each other; especially late-Winter – Spring.

- **Adult size:** In the Northeast, adults often weigh 30-50 lbs., are 4-5 feet long, and ~2 feet tall; is the largest coyote subspecies.
- **Diet:** Widely varied diet including rodents, rabbits, amphibians and reptiles, insects, berries, fruits, and deer fawns.
- First arrived in the Northeast in the 1950s, having migrated eastward and southward from Canada following the human-caused extirpation of Gray Wolves.
- On average share ~25% of their DNA with the Gray Wolf, which is due to breeding with them during their range expansion, and ~10% of their DNA with domestic dogs.
- Dens may consist of a hollowed-out tree stump, rock outcrop, or existing burrow made by Raccoons, skunks, or other medium-sized carnivores. Will also excavate dens themselves.
- Only use dens to give birth to pups (typically between 4-8 during April/May) and during the nursing period. Often have several dens so that they can move to another if one gets fleas and/or parasites or is compromised to predators.
- The adult pair and the pups stay together until the pups disperse in late-Fall; sometimes a helper sibling from the previous litter will stay and help take care of the next litter.
- Pups may disperse 50+ miles, especially in areas where coyote densities are high and also in heavily human-developed areas.
- Use a variety of vocalizations (howling, yipping, etc.) and scent marking to define their territory.

Bobcat

Lynx rufus

ALL NORTHEAST STATES

Where: Mainly in forested areas, around swamps, and rocky ledges. Also suburban areas with sizable forest tracts.

Tips: Rarely seen by people due to being very wary and well-camouflaged. Look for their tracks in mud or snow as evidence of their presence.

- **Adult size:** Males average ~20 lbs. and females average ~15 lbs. Are 30-36 in. long and 18-22 in. tall at shoulder height.

- **Diet:** Primarily eat rabbits as well as squirrels, mice, skunks, opossums, birds, and snakes.

- Named for their short ("bobbed"), 5-6 inch length tail.

- Are largely solitary, only coming together to mate and when the female is with her kittens.

- Female has ~1-4 kittens in her litter, and births and raises them herself in a den which can be in a rock crevice or a cave, under a rocky ledge, in a brush pile, or in a hollowed-out tree or stump; often will use the same den site multiple years in a row.

- Size of adult's home range (the area over which they live) can be from a few square miles to over 100 square miles; areas of poorer habitat quality typically result in larger home ranges.

- They mark their territory using feces, urine, and anal glands fluid, which are deposited on logs, rocks, stumps, and other elevated and exposed surfaces to maximize scent dispersal.

- Are great climbers and often climb trees to rest, chase prey, and/or escape predators.

- Widespread and relatively common throughout much of the Northeast; rarely seen as a result of being very wary of people.

Red Fox

Vulpes vulpes   ALL NORTHEAST STATES

Where: Prefer areas where forests abut fields, meadows, or orchards.

Tips: If you have chickens, make sure to provide secure coops, both from potential entry from above and below by predators such as foxes.

- **Adult size:** 8-15 lbs., 22-34 in. long, and 15-16 in. tall at shoulder height. Their tail is often ~70% the length of their body.
- **Diet:** Have a varied diet; primarily eat small mammals, birds (especially those that spend a lot of time on the ground), amphibians and reptiles, insects, and ripening fruits.
- Widely distributed; found throughout most of North America, Europe, Asia, northern Africa, and southern ~2/3rds of Australia.
- Most often will remain with their same mate for life.
- Make dens in the middle of the Winter where they will birth and raise their young ("pups"); average ~4-5 pups in their litter, though can have as many as 13.
- Most commonly construct dens by digging an ~15-20 foot-long burrow underground, often expanding previous burrows or tunnels made by Woodchucks and Skunks. Also den in barns, abandoned sheds, under decks, and in rock crevices.
- Have vertically-slit pupils, which enables them good vision across a range of lighting conditions.
- Often will "cache" (store by hiding) extra food by digging a hole and burying it, to come back to eat at a later date.
- Make a wide variety of vocalizations including barks, howls, and whines.

Gray Fox

Urocyon cinereoargenteus   ALL NORTHEAST STATES

Where: Primarily found in dense deciduous forests within thicket areas and around swamps.

Tips: Rarely seen given their nocturnal activity patterns and propensity for living in heavily vegetated areas.

- **Adult size:** Slightly smaller than the Red Fox. Adults are 7-14 lbs., 20-30 in. long, and 12-17 in. tall at shoulder height. Their tail is often ~70% the length of their body.

- **Diet:** Have a varied diet; primarily eat small mammals, birds, amphibians and reptiles, insects, acorns, corn, and fruits.

- The only member of the Canid (dog) Family in North America which can readily climb trees. They have semi-retractable claws, which is a climbing adaptation.

- Hunt in areas with more vegetative/shrub cover than where Red Foxes hunt. Additionally, they often hunt in trees, actively jumping from branch to branch in the tree crown.

- Most often will remain with their same mate for life.

- Often return to the same den site year-after-year. Dens often are in hollow trees or logs, in rock crevices, under barns, in abandoned sheds, up in trees, or in dense vegetation.

- Spend the daytime in their den and are active outside of the den from late-evening until dawn.

- Are more aggressive than Red Foxes; because of this and that they can climb trees, coyotes have less of an impact on their populations than coyotes do on Red Fox populations.

- Unlike the Red Fox, the Gray Fox is resistant to mange, a mite that causes skin irritation which often leads to death.

Beaver

Castor canadensis   All Northeast States

Where: Mainly within expansive wetlands that they create by damming streams and brooks, especially those immediately abutted by their preferred tree species *(see below)*.

Tips: Can be seen swimming and feeding during dusk and dawn near their lodges.

- **Adult size:** The largest rodent in North America (can reach ~65 lbs.). Are 2-3 feet long with a 10-18 in. tail.

- **Diet:** Eat a variety of aquatic plants, favoring water lilies, and all different parts of woody plants. Inner bark of trees and shrubs, particularly aspen, birch, willow, alder, and red maple are their most preferred, and comprise much of their Winter diet.

- Their large front teeth grow continuously throughout their life.

- Have a number of aquatic adaptations including: 1) webbed rear feet that help them swim; 2) large lungs that allow them to stay underwater for up to ~15 minutes; 3) large, flattened tails that they steer with; 4) transparent eyelids which act as goggles underwater; 5) nostrils that can close when underwater.

- Also use their tails for communication (by slapping them on the water), for fat storage, and to prop themselves up with.

- Impressive engineers, weaving together sticks and packing with mud, their dams can turn a small stream into a large wetland.

- Live in a lodge that they build, which can be of two types: 1) the most common type is made out of sticks, mud, and rocks, and 2) the less common type is a lodge dug into the bank of a river, stream, or a steep-banked and deep pond or lake.

- Have a sizeable living chamber within their lodge, which is above the water-line and with one or two underwater entrances.

NORTH AMERICAN RIVER OTTER

Lontra canadensis   ALL NORTHEAST STATES

Where: Rivers, streams, ponds, lakes, and marshes with abundant herbaceous plant life.

Tips: In Winter, look for evidence in the snow of their "slides" (wide troughs along the edges of wetlands), especially near rivers and streams.

- **Adult size:** 10-30 lbs. and 36-45 in. long. Males tend to be notably larger than females.

- **Diet:** Have a varied diet often including fish, crayfish, amphibians, reptiles, birds and bird eggs, and aquatic plants.

- Have a number of swimming-related adaptations including: 1) all four feet being webbed, 2) the ability to close their nostrils and ears, 3) a flattened and strongly-muscled tail.

- Their long and very sensitive whiskers help them find food underwater, especially when the water is murky/cloudy.

- Able to stay underwater for as long as ~4 minutes.

- Have litters typically comprised of 1-3 young (called "kits") born in a den, which often are abandoned Beaver lodges or in natural cavities and abandoned burrows of other animals.

- Kits will remain with mother for up to one year before leaving to set-up their own territory elsewhere.

- Primarily nocturnal, but can be seen during the daytime playing or feeding, especially more so during the Winter.

- Otter "slides" are places where they slide on their bellies, often in mud or in snow, mainly for the purposes of playing and for efficiently travelling between neighboring wetlands.

- Populations in the Northeast declined throughout the 1800s due to a combination of habitat loss and over-hunting; their numbers have recovered considerably since that time.

NORTH AMERICAN PORCUPINE

Erethizon dorsatum   ALL NORTHEAST STATES

Where: Forested areas, often those with some coniferous trees and/or access to fruit trees.

Tips: Look for large piles of their fecal pellets ("poop") at the base of hollow standing trees as evidence of their presence.

- **Adult size:** The 2nd-largest rodent in North America (the Beaver is the largest). Adults often weigh ~20 lbs. and are 2-3 feet long.

- **Diet:** Spend much of their time in trees feeding. Primarily eat evergreen needles and the inner bark of trees during the Winter and more of green plants, fruits, seeds, leaves, and roots during the rest of the year.

- Covered in ~30,000 quills, which are everywhere on their body except for their belly area. These quills are modified hair which are made from keratin, the same protein that comprises much of our finger/toenails.

- They can't shoot their quills. They raise their quills when feeling threatened and can detach them easily when they are touched.

- Active year-round, though during bad weather in the Winter they may den, either by themselves or with other porcupines, in structures such as hollow trees, caves, or decaying logs.

- Typically give birth to just a single baby (called a "porcupette") after a 7-month gestation period; very rarely have twins.

- Are very vocal and make a wide variety of sounds including shrieks, grunts, wails, and howls.

- Are good swimmers; their hollow quills make them buoyant.

- Often are drawn to roadsides during the Winter and early-Spring to obtain salt (such as road de-icing salt) and salt-rich vegetation, which leads to many being killed by vehicles.

FISHER
Martes pennanti   ALL NORTHEAST STATES

Where: Areas of extensive, contiguous, closed canopy forest.

Tips: Rarely seen due to their nocturnal activity and their secretive nature; look for their tracks in snow or mud as evidence of their presence.

- **Adult size:** Males (8-15 lbs. and up to ~3 feet long) are notably larger than females (3-7 lbs. and up to ~2 feet long).

- **Diet:** Eat a wide range of mammals such as squirrels, rabbits, mice, shrews; also birds and a variety of nuts, berries, and fruits. Is the only mammal in the Northeast that is regularly able to successfully kill and eat porcupines.

- They do not eat fish, contrary to what their name suggests. It is believed that their name originated from European settlers who noted their resemblance to a "European polecat" which is also known as a "fichet" or "fitche".

- Are predominantly solitary, aside from when a female is raising her young ("kits") by herself, and when a male and female come together briefly to mate.

- The second-largest member of the weasel family found in the Northeast (the North American River Otter is the largest).

- Have wide feet that help them walk better in deep snow.

- Partially retractable claws help them to be agile climbers.

- Populations declined considerably throughout the Northeast during the 1800s through the early-1900s primarily due to habitat loss (via clearing of forests) and over-exploitation from trapping. Their populations have recovered substantially since that time due to reforestation as well as from a number of successful re-introduction programs.

Long-Tailed Weasel

Mustela frenata ALL NORTHEAST STATES

Where: A variety of habitats ranging from open forests, to shrublands, to forest-field edges.

Tips: Make sure to secure chicken coops well from these very nimble and wily predators.

- **Adult size:** Males average ~0.5 lbs. and females ~0.25 lbs. Typically between 11-17 in. long, with a 3-6 in. long tail. Males tend to be a bit longer and with longer tails than females.

- **Diet:** Primarily eat small mammals, such as mice and voles, though will also eat mammals larger than themselves including rabbits, squirrels, and chipmunks. Will also eat birds and bird eggs (including domestic chickens and eggs), and fruits and berries.

- Hunt any time of the day or night, though most of their hunting takes place at night; are active year-round.

- Are fast on the ground, adept climbers, and good swimmers.

- Hunt on the ground, in trees, or in small mammal burrows underground; often eat ~$1/3^{rd}$ of their body weight daily.

- Dens are often within rock piles, hollow logs, old buildings/barns; sometimes will take over an existing den after killing the prior den resident. A nearby water source is an important element in selecting den sites.

- Often have multiple den sites throughout their home range (the area over which they live), which averages ~75-100 acres.

- Are solitary aside from the time period when raising young.

- Coat changes to entirely white (with black tail tip) in Winter.

Woodchuck

Marmota monax   ALL NORTHEAST STATES

Where: Mainly open areas such as fields, meadows, orchards, as well as open forests.

Tips: Consider fencing your vegetable garden to reduce Woodchuck grazing.

- **Adult size:** 4-12 lbs., 16-26 in. long, with a 4-6 in. long tail.
- **Diet:** Eat a wide variety of vegetation, namely fruits, herbs, flowers, shrubs, and many different agricultural crops.
- The name "Woodchuck" is derived from the Cree word "wuchak", which refers to somewhat similar looking species including the Fisher and weasels.
- Construct impressive burrow/tunnel system which often has 5+ entrances, is up to ~45 feet long, and is typically 2-5 feet deep.
- There is a nesting chamber located at the end of the main tunnel which is used for sleeping and for raising their young. Also have a separate toilet chamber (or "latrine"); once it is full they will seal it off and dig another latrine chamber.
- Often will have two burrows: a Summer burrow, usually in open areas (such as fields, meadows, pastures) and a Winter burrow, typically in a wooded setting that often goes below the frost line. Will seal off their Winter burrow entrances with dirt once they have entered and have begun their hibernation.
- Female litter is often comprised of 2-6 young ("pups", "kits", "cubs", or "chucklings"); mother raises them for 2-3 months.
- Are true hibernators, unlike Black Bears *(page 64)*. During hibernation their heart rate drops from ~100 down to < 10 beats per minute, breathing rate reduces considerably, and body temperature drops from 97° F down to as low as ~40° F.

Raccoon
Procyon lotor   ALL NORTHEAST STATES

Where: Found in almost any setting, ranging from forests to dense urban areas, and almost any type of setting in-between.

Tips: Make sure to secure your outdoor garbage and compost containers to keep Raccoons out.

- **Adult size:** Are commonly 12-35 lbs. (though some individuals exceed 50 lbs.), 24-38 in. long, with an 8-16 in. long tail.

- **Diet:** Have an extremely varied diet including insects, aquatic invertebrates, turtles and their eggs, Muskrat kits, birds and their eggs, nuts, seeds, berries, and often get into garbage cans, eat chicken feed and eggs, agricultural crops, and more.

- Females give birth to ~1-7 young ("cubs") in their den typically in April/May. Den sites often are hollow trees, but can also be brush piles, deep rock crevices, caves, and inside sheds/barns.

- The mother nurses her cubs for ~6 weeks, and they often stay with her until the following Spring.

- Outside of when cubs are being raised by their mother, Raccoons are solitary. However, during very cold weather in the Winter, multiple individuals may den together to conserve heat.

- Have great dexterity and very sensitive hands, which they use to obtain prey, such as crayfish under rocks, and are great climbers and swimmers.

- Their name is derived from the Algonquin word "arakun", which means "he scratches with his hands".

- Can rotate their hind feet as much as 180-degrees which helps them to dexterously descend trees head-first.

- Rabies was first identified in Raccoons in the Northeast in the early-1990s; they and bats are the primary carriers of the disease in the region, though they carry different strains.

Virginia Opossum

Didelphis virginiana   ALL NORTHEAST STATES

Where: Found in almost any setting ranging from forests to dense urban areas, and almost any setting in-between.

Tips: Watch out for opossums, and other wildlife, when you are driving.

- **Adult size:** 4-12 lbs., 2-3 feet long with a 10-20 in. long tail.
- **Diet:** Widely varied diet mainly including insects, worms, small mammals, birds, bird eggs, nuts, seeds, fruit, and carrion.
- Their name is derived from the Algonquin word "apassum", which means "white animal" or "white beast".
- The only marsupial in the U.S.; most marsupials (mammals that carry young in a pouch) are in Australia and South America.
- Females have ~1-13 "kits" in a litter; size of a jelly bean at birth.
- Kits immediately crawl into their mother's pouch when born and remain there for ~8 weeks nursing; they then largely ride on the mother's back for the next ~4 weeks *(see photo above)*.
- Opossums are good climbers and swimmers. They use their prehensile tail to stabilize themselves when walking on branches, and the first toe on their hind feet is opposable (similar to a thumb) which helps them to be very agile climbers.
- When they feel threatened they fall over and pretend to be dead (is where the phrase "playing possum" comes from).
- Have the most teeth (50 teeth) of any U.S. land mammal; show their teeth when they feel threatened, and also hiss and growl.
- Because they have a lower body temperature (94-97°F) than mammals (97-103°F), the rabies virus is rarely able to survive in their body.

Striped Skunk

Mephites mephites   All Northeast States

Where: Found in almost any setting ranging from forests to dense urban areas, and almost any setting in-between.

Tips: Make sure to secure your outdoor garbage and compost containers well to keep skunks out of these.

- **Adult size:** 5-14 lbs., 21-26 in. long, with an 8-11 in. long tail; roughly the size of a house cat. Are only 5-8 in. tall at shoulder height (much shorter than most people think that they are).

- **Diet:** Eat a wide range of plants and animals including a variety of vegetation, insects, beetles, crickets, earthworms, bird eggs, turtle eggs, small mammals, and will get into people's garbage.

- A male is a "buck", female is a "doe", and baby is a "kit".

- Female will give birth typically to ~6-7 young ("kits") in a den in mid-Winter, and will often stay with her until late-Summer.

- Most often don't excavate their own den but will den in an abandoned burrow from another animal, in a hollow under a tree, under a shed or porch, or in a similar such setting.

- Spray potential predators with a foul-smelling oily musk which, if it gets in the eyes, can be painful to the sprayed individual and can even cause temporary blindness.

- Can spray 10-15 feet, which can be detected up to a mile away.

- Have a strong sense of smell, long claws, and sharp teeth, all of which are all helpful in finding and digging up insects and for tearing apart rotting logs and stumps in their search for food.

- They do not hibernate, though during long stretches of cold weather in the Winter will remain in their den and largely inactive, sometimes with other skunks to conserve heat. Often lose ~30% of their body weight over the Winter.

Eastern Cottontail

Sylvilagus floridanus   All Northeast States

Introduced Species

Where: Open areas like fields, meadows, orchards, and yards.

Tips: Watch rabbit(s) in your yard, from afar, during any Spring-Summer evening to see where the nest may be. Don't disturb the nest if you find where it is.

- **Adult size:** 2-3 lbs. and 14-18 in. long.

- **Diet:** Eat a wide range of herbaceous plants and grasses, and often raid vegetable gardens. In Winter, will often eat stems and buds of woody plants, especially those of berries and fruits.

- Introduced to the Northeast in the late-1800s. Are native to the eastern U.S. in regions south of the Northeast and west through much of the midwestern and southern U.S.

- New England Cottontail is the native rabbit in the region; declined markedly during 1900's due to loss of thicket habitat, and competition with White-Tailed Deer and Eastern Cottontail.

- Each female typically has 2-4 litters in a given year, each of which consists of ~4-6 young (called "kittens"). In the Northeast, litters are typically born March-August.

- Female makes a nest by scratching out a depression in the ground, which can be up to a foot deep, and lines the nest with dried grass and also fur that she pulls from her body.

- The mother returns to the nest during dusk and dawn to nurse the young, and stays away the rest of the day and night, so as to not attract predators to the nest. She will do so until they are ~3-5 weeks old, after which they are left to fend on their own.

- Sometimes will eat their own fecal pellets ("poop") to increase their vitamins and minerals levels; known as "coprophagia".

LITTLE BROWN BAT
Myotis lucifugus   ALL NORTHEAST STATES

Where: Roost in buildings and tree cavities in the warmer months; overwinter in caves and mines.

Tips: Watch in the evening sky for bats during Summer months.

- **Adult size:** Weigh 1/8-1/2 an ounce, with a body length of 2.5-4 in., and a wingspan of 9-11 in.

- **Diet:** Predominantly hunt large swarms of insects, and eat ~½ of their body weight in insects each night; nursing females may eat their entire body weight, or more, of food per night.

- Use echolocation to detect and to catch their prey.

- Female raises a single young (a "pup") by herself, and nurses it for ~4 weeks; by then the pup has reached adult weight, is able to fly, can hunt, and becomes independent of its mother.

- Use 3 different roost types throughout the year including: 1) daytime roosts; 2) nocturnal roosts (often in attics), where they often roost in large aggregations overnight; and 3) hibernation roosts, typically in caves and abandoned mines where the temperatures remain above freezing and have high humidity. Sometimes a fourth type of roost, a "nursery roost", is used by an individual female raising her young.

- Populations (of this and other bat species) in the Northeast have declined by more than 90% since the discovery of new fungus in 2007 in some of their overwintering caves in New York State; this fungus has spread widely throughout their range since then.

- Infection by this fungus (termed "White-Nose Syndrome", due to a white-growth that appears on the nose of some infected individuals) causes them to become active in the Winter, when they should be hibernating, and often leads to starvation.

EASTERN GRAY SQUIRREL

Sciurus carolinensis   ALL NORTHEAST STATES

Where: Deciduous forests and suburban and urban areas that contain nut-producing trees.

Tips: There are two common color morphs, gray and black, and rarely all-white ones will occur; these are all the same species.

- **Adult size:** Adults are 1-1.5 lbs., 15-21 in. long, with a 5-10 in. long tail.
- **Diet:** Most of their diet is comprised of a variety of nuts; also eat berries, mushrooms, flowers, roots, fruits, seeds, and buds.
- Live in dens/nests that are often either in tree cavities or ones that they construct out of leaves and twigs high up in trees.
- Often will live with other individuals in dens/nests, though females will kick out male(s) once she gives birth to young.
- Females typically have two litters of young ("kits") each year; one in early-Spring and the other in early-to-mid-Summer; each litter typically has ~2-7 kits.
- Female often mates with multiple males during a breeding event, and the young of each litter often have a mix of fathers.
- Tend to run in a zig-zag pattern to avoid predators; though this is maladaptive when trying to avoid cars when crossing roads.
- They "cache" (store by hiding) large numbers of nuts by burying them underground to come back to eat later; a single squirrel can cache up to ~10,000 nuts in a given year.
- Because they don't retrieve many nuts that they bury, they act as an effective tree planter/disperser due to many of those nuts growing into trees (such as acorns growing into oak trees).

American Red Squirrel

Tamiasciurus hudsonicus   ALL NORTHEAST STATES

Where: Prefer mixed forests that contain coniferous trees.

Tips: Listen for their distinctive loud trills and chatter sounds as an effective way to identify their presence.

- **Adult size:** Are ~1/2 the size of Eastern Gray Squirrels. Weigh 7-10 oz., are 10-14 in. long, with a 3.5-6 in. long tail.
- **Diet:** Eat a variety of nuts, seeds, and fruit; their most preferred food is fresh seeds from within cones of conifer trees.
- Active year-round, with much of their Winter activity occurring mid-day to coincide with the warmest temperatures.
- Store large numbers of unopened cones in "middens" as a Winter food source. Their midden is a large pile of chewed-off cone scales at the base of a cone-bearing tree, which provides a cool and moist storage area for unopened cones which keeps the cones from opening and releasing their seeds.
- Middens are typically 2-3 feet wide and ~1 foot deep, though can be up to 10 feet wide and ~2 feet deep. Will often have several middens in their territory, which they fiercely defend.
- Middens may contain thousands of unopened cones, and an individual Red Squirrel may eat seeds from upwards of 50 cones per day from a midden.
- Chew into Sugar Maple trees and then return later to consume the sap that has dripped on branches and down the trunk.
- Are very vocal and use a wide range of noises for various communication purposes. Will sometimes use a different alarm call for aerial predators (a high frequency call) compared to the call used for terrestrial predators (more of a bark-like call).

Southern Flying Squirrel

Glaucomys volans   All Northeast States

Where: Mature deciduous and mixed forests that contain an abundant amount of nut-producing trees.

Tips: Due to being nocturnal and quite secretive, they are very rarely seen by people.

- **Adult size:** Approximately one-half the size of American Red Squirrels and one-quarter the size of Eastern Gray Squirrels. Weigh 1.5-3 oz., are 8-10 in. long with a 3-4 in. long tail.

- **Diet:** Eat acorns, nuts, seeds, lichens, mushrooms, berries, sap, insects, and sometimes small birds and their eggs.

- There are two species of flying squirrel in the Northeast, the Northern Flying Squirrel and the Southern Flying Squirrel; they have very similar life-histories.

- Have a folded layer of loose skin between their front and back legs that they spread out to glide down in the air with.

- Can cover 150+ feet horizontally and reach up to ~30 mph during a single glide.

- Slow themselves down just prior to landing by raising their tail and leaning their body back/upwards.

- Typically live and nest in standing dead trees ("snags"), former woodpecker holes, birdhouses, and abandoned bird and squirrel nests. Can fit into a hole the size of a quarter. Sometimes will share a nest with another pair.

- Nocturnal; most active from ~2 hours after sunset to ~2 hours before sunrise.

- Have very large eyes which enable them to see well at night.

- Sometimes aggregate into single-sex groups (called "huddles") for warmth during the Winter; can contain up to 20 individuals.

Eastern Chipmunk

Tamias striatus　　　　　　　ALL NORTHEAST STATES

Where: Found in a wide variety of landscape settings ranging from forests, to fields and meadows, to yards.

Tips: Listen for their high-pitched "chip" calls and their loud and repeated "munk" calls to identify their presence.

- **Adult size:** Weigh 2-5 oz., are 3-4.5 in. long, and with a tail slightly shorter than their body length.
- **Diet:** Eat a variety of nuts, seeds, fruits, berries, mushrooms, worms, insects, amphibians, bird eggs, and some baby birds.
- Are solitary aside from when the female is raising her young.
- Spend most of their life underground in burrows that can be up to 30 feet long and 3 feet deep. Burrows typically have an upper level, lined with vegetation such as grass and leaves for insulation, and is where the chipmunks sleep, and a lower level which is where they store nuts and seeds for the Winter; sometimes store upwards of a gallon of nuts and seeds.
- They do not hibernate; instead are in a state known as "torpor" for a few-to-several days at a time during Winter, whereby their resting heart rate may drop to less than 10 beats per minute, down from ~350 beats per minute. They then "awaken" to feed briefly before going back into torpor. Are unable to hibernate throughout the Winter because they cannot build up enough fat reserves to last them through an entire Winter.
- Females typically produce two litters of "pups" per year, one in early-Spring and one in mid-Summer, with 2-6 pups per litter.
- They breathe very fast, averaging ~75 breaths per minute. As a comparison, humans average ~12-16 breaths per minute.
- Can live up to ~8 years in the wild; most live less than 3 years.

Muskrat

Ondatra zibethicus   ALL NORTHEAST STATES

Where: Almost any freshwater wetland type, especially ones with cattails; sometimes brackish wetlands.

Tips: Due to being primarily nocturnal and skittish, seeing their lodges/huts is often the best evidence of their presence.

- **Adult size:** Average ~3 lbs., with a body length of ~12 in., and an ~10 in. long, scaly, and vertically-flattened tail.

- **Diet:** Primarily eat stems and roots of aquatic vegetation as well as insects, crayfish, and dead fish.

- Named for the musky-smelling secretion that they emit for the purposes of communication and for attracting mates.

- Use their tail as a "rudder" to steer when swimming, and have partially-webbed hind feet which they propel themselves with.

- Primarily swim on the surface; if disturbed, will dive underwater and can stay under for as long as 15-20 minutes.

- Construct small structures ("lodges") in the water near shore made from soft vegetation that they live in with a nesting chamber inside that is above the water line with one or multiple underwater entrances. Also create burrows/tunnels in soil along the shore banks that they will live in, especially along streams and canals. Sometimes will live in abandoned beaver lodges.

- Often will have one primary "lodge" that they will spend most of their time in and other smaller ones, called "feeding huts", that they will spend a lesser amount of time in and, as the name suggests, will primarily use when eating/feeding.

- Active year-round and throughout the day and night; more active at night. Less active during colder spells in Winter and spend much of those times in their lodge.

Star-Nosed Mole
Condylura cristata   ALL NORTHEAST STATES

Where: Found in wet soils adjacent to a variety of wetland types such as ponds, marshes, streams, and vernal pools.

Tips: Locally common; very rarely seen due to living almost entirely underground and underwater.

- **Adult size:** Weigh 1-2.5 oz. and are 6-8 in. long.
- **Diet:** Eat a wide range of invertebrates, as well as some small amphibians and small fish.
- Have 22 fleshy tentacles extending from their snout in the shape of a star, which is approximately the size of a human fingertip; they use this primarily for detecting prey.
- Combined, these tentacles contain ~100,000 nerve fibers; for comparison, an entire human hand has ~17,000 nerve fibers.
- The world's fastest eater; are able to detect and ingest a prey item in ~¼ of a second.
- Eat prey while underground or underwater.
- One of only two mammal species in the world that are known to be able to smell underwater (the Water Shrew is the other). They do this by quickly blowing air bubbles underwater and then sucking them back in to smell for prey.
- Have strong front legs and shoulders and paddle-like front feet; features that help them be strong swimmers and diggers.
- Active year-round, throughout the day and night, and are even seen swimming underneath ice.
- Their extensive tunneling aerates soil and helps provide much needed oxygen to the roots of plants in wet/saturated soils. Each individual often creates ~100-150 feet of tunnels per day.

MEADOW VOLE

Microtus pennsylvanicus   ALL NORTHEAST STATES

Where: Open settings such as meadows, agricultural fields, grass and sedge marshes, and yards.

Tips: Look for evidence of their burrows through the snow when snow melts to the point where you can see some grass.

- **Adult size:** Weigh 1-2 oz., are 4.5-6.5 in. long, with a 1.5-2.5 in. long tail.

- **Diet:** Grasses, sedges, and a wide variety of herbaceous plants; eat tree bark and roots in Winter.

- Create extensive burrow systems including in the snow.

- Active year-round; more active during the daytime in Winter and during nighttime in warmer periods of the year.

- May live between a year and a year-and-a-half, though most live only a few months or so.

- Females sexually mature as early as 25 days-old and 40 days-old for males.

- Female may have as many as 8 litters in a given year. A female's litter is often fathered by multiple males.

- A litter typically consists of ~4-6 young ("pups"), though can contain as many as 12.

- The female does the entirety of raising of the pups, raising them in a nest made of grass, leaves, and plant material.

- Pups use "ultrasonic calling" to communicate with their mother, for example when they've accidentally wandered from the nest; the mother hears this and retrieves them. Ultrasonic calling occurs at high frequencies that are inaudible to the human ear.

AMPHIBIANS

Amphibians have the lowest species diversity in the region among the four groups in this book. A total of 24 amphibian species are present in the Northeast, which are equally represented between frogs and toads (12 species) and salamanders and newts (12 species). They are all "ecothermic" or "cold-blooded", which means that they depend on external environmental conditions/temperatures to regulate their body temperature. This means they are primarily inactive during the colder months. Additionally, all amphibians share the risk of drying out and, as a result, have developed a range of behavioral and physiological adaptations to ensure that they remain adequately hydrated.

The life histories of Northeast amphibians are quite diverse, primarily with respect to the different habitat types, driven by both breeding habits and competition for resources. For example, some amphibian species in the region breed in permanent standing bodies of freshwater, some breed in wetlands that only hold water for a portion of the year, some breed in streams and/or rivers, and two salamander species breed entirely on land.

Ten amphibian species are included in this book, which comprise approximately 40% of the 24 amphibian species present in the Northeast. Six frog/toad species and four salamander species are included, and most of those that were selected for inclusion are those that are the most common in the region; one exception is the Eastern Spadefoot, which was included due to its very unique natural history.

While amphibians are a group that don't tend to attract as much attention from the general public as mammals or birds do, you'll find through reading the next 10 pages how absolutely fascinating they truly are!

WOOD FROG
Lithobates sylvaticus   ALL NORTHEAST STATES

Where: Breed in vernal pools; spend the remainder of the year on and amongst leaf litter in the surrounding uplands.

Tips: Listen for choruses of males (sounds like a bunch of ducks quacking) calling from vernal pools on warm, sunny days in early-Spring.

- **Adult size:** ~1.5-2.5 in. long.

- **Clutch details:** Eggs are individually contained as a jelly-like spherical mass of up to ~3,000 eggs per female. Within a day after deposition, after swelling with water, are roughly the size of a softball. Often many females deposit their egg masses side-by-side forming "rafts" containing hundreds or more of masses.

- **Call description:** Sounds very similar to Mallards *(page 16)* quacking. Males call when floating on the surface of the water.

- The only frog found north of the Arctic Circle in North America.

- Can survive freezing for weeks at a time due to an adaptation whereby they produce an anti-freeze-like substance in their body; specifically, their cells fill with high concentrations of glucose (a type of liquid sugar that is resistant to freezing). In Winter, 30%+ of their body may freeze and turn to ice.

- Upon hatching, sibling tadpoles can recognize one another and often congregate together (a "safety-in-numbers" behavior).

- Males have notably thicker thumbs and bulkier forearms than females; these are adaptations that help him hold on to the female during egg deposition by grasping her underneath her body (in front of her forelimbs) and intertwining his thumbs together holding on tight, aided also by his strong forearms.

- Their Latin name means "one that walks (or haunts) amidst the trees" and refers to them living mainly in forests and woodlands.

American Bullfrog

Lithobates catesbeianus   ALL NORTHEAST STATES

Where: Found along shorelines of ponds, lakes, and reservoirs; occasionally encountered away from these wetlands during feeding movements.

Tips: Listen for their very loud "jug-o-rum" calls at large wetlands during late-Spring – mid-Summer.

- **Adult size:** ~4-8 in. long; the largest frog in North America.
- **Clutch details:** Each female lays ~10,000 – 20,000 eggs within a large mat that can be up to 2 feet wide; the mat floats at the surface initially and then subsequently sinks to the bottom.
- **Call description:** A very loud call that sounds like "jug-o-rum".
- Eat almost any animal smaller than they are including a variety of insects, fish, other frogs, recently hatched turtles, rodents, and small snakes and birds; also some vegetation.
- Tadpoles take 2 – 3 years until they metamorphose into a frog.
- Overwinter at the bottom of wetlands that have sufficient dissolved oxygen, which is absorbed through their skin.
- You can tell the gender from the size of the "tympanum" (the circular patch behind each eye, which is analogous to an eardrum); the male's tympanum is equal to or greater than the size of each of his eyes *(see photo above)*, whereas the female's tympanum is smaller than each of her eyes.
- Have powerful hind legs; can jump as far as 15 body lengths.
- Sometimes emit a long, loud, high-pitch scream when grabbed.
- Were introduced to a number of areas in the U.S. from the release of individuals reared for classroom lab dissections.

Spring Peeper

Pseudacris crucifer   All Northeast States

Where: Breed in almost any type of freshwater wetland. Spend the remainder of the year in the surrounding uplands.

Tips: Listen for their very loud choruses on Spring nights; may include thousands of males calling at a single wetland.

- **Adult size:** ~0.7-1.5 in. long.
- **Clutch details:** Each female lays up to ~1,000 eggs each year. Eggs are laid singly, or in small clusters, underwater on aquatic vegetation or directly on the bottom of the wetland.
- **Call description:** A very loud and high-pitched "peep"; also make a trill-like territorial call, which is made when another male is calling too close by.
- Males call by inflating their vocal sac which extends balloon-like from their throat *(see photo above)*.
- Though Spring Peepers are small, their calls are very loud; a chorus of Spring Peepers can be heard from up to a mile away.
- Females tend to select males that have the fastest and loudest calls, which is likely an indicator of the male's fitness.
- Like Gray Treefrogs *(page 93)*, they have adhesive discs on their toes (often called "toe pads"), which they use to scale vertical surfaces such as trees and shrubs.
- Like Gray Treefrogs and Wood Frogs, Spring Peepers can survive at least partial freezing by producing an anti-freeze like liquid in their bodies *(see discussion in Wood Frog, page 90)*.
- Known as "Pinkletink" on Martha's Vineyard, "Tinkletoes" in New Brunswick, and "Pink-Winks" in some parts of Nova Scotia.

Gray Treefrog

Hyla versicolor — ALL NORTHEAST STATES

Where: Breed primarily in wetlands with woody shrubs and/or dead trees within the wetland. Spend the remainder of the year in forested uplands.

Tips: Listen, in May/June, for choruses of their melodic trills from wetlands.

- **Adult size:** ~1.5-2 in. long.

- **Clutch details:** Each female lays up to ~2,000 eggs in small, loose clusters (each typically containing < 50 eggs) attached underwater to aquatic vegetation.

- **Call description:** A loud, short trill.

- Like Spring Peepers *(page 92)*, they have adhesive discs on their toes (called "toe pads") which they use to scale vertical surfaces such as trees, shrubs, houses, barns, and buildings.

- Outside of when they are breeding, they spend the rest of the year predominantly in trees under bark and in tree cavities. Sometimes found using birdhouses and inside of gutters.

- Sometimes found on windows and on the sides of houses next to outdoor lights that are kept on at night, due to an abundance of prey (moths, insects, etc.) that are attracted to the light.

- Adults are predominantly gray with dark markings; have some ability to change color (light green, gray, brown) to blend with the background. Young are bright lime green when they emerge from the wetlands in Summer; are well-camouflaged in the green vegetation and foliage of the season.

- Tadpoles may develop bright red tails, typically as a response to stress (such as high predator densities); believed to redirect attacks to their tail rather than to their less-expendable body.

American Toad

Anaxyrus americanus   All Northeast States

Where: Breed in almost any type of freshwater wetland. Spend the rest of the year in a wide range of upland types.

Tips: Listen for their long, high-pitched trills coming from wetlands in mid-to-late Spring.

- **Adult size:** ~2-4 in. long.
- **Clutch details:** Each female lays ~2,000-20,000 eggs each year, which are deposited in long, paired, spaghetti-like strands draped over submerged vegetation in shallow water.
- **Call description:** A musical trill that typically lasts ~10 – 20 seconds which the male emits while sitting in, or at the edge of, the water in a breeding wetland.
- The most generalist of all amphibians in the Northeast, both in terms of the variety of wetland types they breed in and the upland habitat types they spend the rest of the year in.
- Periodically shed their skin and will eat it to retain the nutrients.
- Absorb water via a darkened color portion on their lower abdomen, called a "seat patch"; absorb up to 70% of their water intake from this.
- Ants make up a large portion of their diet and are the main source from which they derive their own toxic secretions (from the formic acid present in ants) as defense against predators.
- You can't get warts from toads, that is a myth. However, due to their skin secretions, hand-washing is recommended following handling of a toad (especially before you eat).
- Males emit a "release call", resembling quiet chirping, when misidentified and grasped by another male in a mistaken mating attempt.

EASTERN SPADEFOOT
Scaphiopus holbrookii CT, MA, RI

Where: Breed in wetlands that dry up each year and that may not have water some years. Live in a range of upland habitats, as long as there is loose/sandy soil for them to burrow in.

Tips: Rarely encountered; are most active during very heavy rain events.

- **Adult size:** ~1.75-2.5 in. long.

- **Clutch details:** Each female deposits ~1,000-2,500 eggs; laid in strands draped over submerged vegetation or directly on the unvegetated bottom of the wetland.

- **Call description:** A loud, low-pitch, nasally-sounding "grunt"; sounds very similar to the "er" call in the old Budweiser frog commercials from the mid-to-late 1990s.

- Named for a "spade-like" growth on the bottom of each hind foot; use these to burrow underground with. This is made of keratin, the same protein that human nails are made from.

- Aside from rare exceptions, are only active aboveground at night.

- The only amphibian in the Northeast with vertically-slit pupils (like the eyes of cats and foxes); their pupils fully dilate at night, giving them very powerful nighttime vision.

- Unlike all other amphibians in the Northeast, they do not breed every year; typically breed when major rain events flood certain wetland basins that are normally dry most of the year and/or don't have water at all during some years.

- Have among the fastest embryonic and larval development rates of any vertebrate in the world, proceeding from newly fertilized egg to emerging juvenile in as short as two weeks.

Spotted Salamander

Ambystoma maculatum   All Northeast States

Where: Breed almost exclusively in freshwater wetlands without predatory fish; spend the rest of year in neighboring wooded uplands.

Tips: Watch out for them crossing roads on warm, rainy Spring nights during their breeding migrations.

- **Adult size:** ~4.5-9 in. long; one of the largest salamanders in the U.S.

- **Clutch details:** Eggs are contained in a jelly-like matrix and deposited as masses (typically ~50-100 eggs per mass) that absorb water and swell as large as a fist. Matrix can be clear or milky white, and a female often deposits up to four masses.

- Spend most of their life underground in burrows/tunnels of small rodents, coming to the surface during warm, moist nights to feed and during several weeks in early–Spring to breed.

- Each individual has a unique pattern of spots, similar to how every human has unique fingerprints.

- Majority of populations comprised of individuals that only have yellow spots; some populations (mainly in the southern U.S.) have individuals with orange spots on their heads.

- Individuals have been found to live up to ~20 years in the wild and even longer in captivity.

- Have a mutualistic relationship with an algae species that grows inside each egg with each salamander embryo; this algae aids the embryo by increasing oxygen content in the egg and removing waste, while the salamander waste provides a beneficially nitrogen-rich environment for the algae to grow in.

Eastern Red-Backed Salamander

Plethodon cinereus   All Northeast States

Where: Under logs, rocks, and other such debris on the forest floor, primarily in deciduous forests or areas of deciduous trees within mixed forests.

Tips: Readily found under logs on the forest floor in Spring-Fall, except during dry spells.

- **Adult size:** ~2-4 in. long.

- **Clutch details:** Typically lay between ~6-9 eggs (up to 15 eggs) in clusters within natural cavities on or under the ground, often inside or beneath logs and under stones. The female guards the eggs from predators and also makes sure that they stay moist.

- Are three color variations ("morphs"), the most common being the striped or "red-back" morph *(pictured above)*, the relatively common gray or "lead-back" morph (entirely dark gray to black), and the rare "ethrysitic" morph (entirely fire-red).

- They do not have lungs and breathe entirely through their skin.

- The most populous salamander in the Northeast. A 1970s study in New Hampshire estimated the per-acre biomass of this species to be approximately equal to that of all small mammals combined and almost twice that of all birds in the forest.

- Mating occurs primarily in the Fall, when pairs engage in an elaborate courtship "dance" called the "tail-straddling walk"; this involves the female walking behind the male while straddling his tail as he walks, undulates his tail, and leads her over a sperm packet he has deposited, and this often lasts > 1 hour.

- Can detach their tail in response to a predator attack, wherein the separated tail wriggles around for a period of minutes, serving to distract the predator while the salamander escapes.

- Tail and limbs can be regenerated after loss.

Northern Two-Lined Salamander

Eurycea bislineata   All Northeast States

Where: Live mostly in, or on the rocky edges of, streams, brooks, and hillside seepages; adults may stray into moist woods periodically.

Tips: Most readily found under flat rocks at the water's edge in small streams and seepages.

- **Adult size:** ~2.5-4 in. long.

- **Clutch details:** Typically attach 10-20 eggs (though as many as 40+) to the undersides of submerged rocks in flowing water; the female often guards the eggs from predators until they hatch after ~1 month.

- Where found, they tend to be quite abundant; more tolerant of sub-optimal environmental conditions (lower dissolved oxygen levels in the water, higher water temperatures, etc.) than the two other stream-salamander species (Northern Dusky Salamander and Northern Spring Salamander) of the Northeast.

- Like the Eastern Red-Backed Salamander *(page 97)*, they do not have lungs and breathe through their skin.

- Larvae are aquatic and can detect presence of predatory fish via chemical cues in the water; often leads to the larvae hiding under submerged rocks for extended periods of time.

- Larvae remain fully-aquatic, and with external feathery gills, for 1 – 3 years after hatching from the egg.

- Have elaborate courtship dance called the "tail-straddling walk" *(see discussion in Eastern Red-Backed Salamander, page 97)*.

- Adults and juveniles overwinter underground in the area immediately surrounding the stream, likely going deep enough to be below the frost line.

Eastern Newt

Notophthalmus viridescens   ALL NORTHEAST STATES

Where: Juveniles, called "efts" *see below)*, inhabit forests, whereas adults inhabit ponds, lakes, and slow-moving rivers.

Tips: Look for the bright orange efts out and about on the forest floor when you are walking in the woods on a warm, rainy Summer day.

- **Adult size:** ~3-5 in. long.

- **Clutch details:** Female deposits ~200 – 400 eggs, often in subsets of a small number of them curled up burrito-style in leaves at the bottom of wetlands.

- Also well-known as the "Red-Spotted Newt".

- Larvae are aquatic (~2-3 months) and metamorphose into terrestrial juveniles (1 – 3 years), which then subsequently metamorphose into aquatic adults. The juvenile *(pictured above)* is bright orange and commonly known as an "eft". The adult is greenish-brown above, yellow below, and has a vertically-flattened tail to aid in swimming. Both the efts and adults have up to ~21 large red spots on their sides/back and lots of smaller black spots/flecks over their entire body.

- At all life stages they are toxic and unpalatable to most other wildlife. The bright orange coloration of the eft serves as a vivid warning to would-be predators; this is what enables them to be active on the forest floor during the daytime.

- Sometimes a "mating ball" will occur when several males attempt to mate with a single female in a wetland.

- During mating rituals, the male attempts to entice the female with his red-spots and by waving his tail which wafts pheromones (chemical attractants) to attract her with.

Reptiles

Reptiles have the second-lowest species diversity in the region among the four wildlife groups included in this book. There are 31 reptile species found in the Northeast, which are represented by 16 turtles, 14 snakes, and a single lizard species. As with amphibians, all of these species (with partial exception to the Leatherback) depend on external environmental conditions to regulate their body temperature, and thus are only active during warmer portions of the year in the Northeast.

As with the other wildlife groups, the life histories of reptiles of the Northeast are quite diverse. For example, some of the snakes live primarily in more open habitats (such as shrublands and meadows), some live in more forested habitats, and some live mostly in and near freshwater wetlands. Turtles show a similar level of diversity in the habitat they live in; some are entirely marine species and are only found off of the coast of the Northeast in saltwater, one spends most of its life in saltmarsh environments, some spend most of their life in various types of freshwater wetland, and one species (the Eastern Box Turtle) spends the grand majority of its life in woodlands and forests.

Ten reptile species are included in this book, which comprise approximately 1/3rd of the 31 reptiles species in the Northeast. Five snake and five turtle species are included, and most that are included are those that are the most common in the region; two exceptions (Eastern Box Turtle and Eastern Hognose Snake) were included due to their unique natural histories.

Though generally not viewed by the public as being as charismatic as some other animals, reptiles are certainly fascinating creatures as you will learn in the pages ahead!

Eastern Box Turtle

Terrapene carolina   ALL NORTHEAST STATES EXCEPT VT

Where: Live mainly in forests and woodlands; will seek out adjoining open areas, such as powerline rights-of-way and fields/meadows for nesting.

Tips: Watch out for them on roads, particularly during late-afternoons – evenings in June during females' movements to and from nesting sites.

- **Adult size:** ~4.5-7 in. long.

- **Clutch details:** Female typically deposits between ~3-8 eggs underground in a nest that she excavates.

- Have hinges on their underside shell that enables them to close up completely within their shell (hence the name "box" turtle).

- Spend the majority of their life in terrestrial environments, only sometimes seeking out wetlands for hydration and to cool off (often by burrowing in the mud) during the peak Summer heat.

- Often take them ~10 years to reach sexual maturity in the Northeast; some individuals have been documented to live 100+ years in the wild.

- Young hatch from the eggs in ~60 days and most commonly will emerge from the nest in late-Summer/early-Fall, though sometimes will wait until the following Spring to emerge.

- In some instances the female will store the sperm of males for multiple years before fertilizing her eggs with.

- One way to tell males and females apart is that males tend to have red eyes whereas females tend to have brown eyes.

- Illegal collection for the pet trade has dramatically reduced their populations throughout their range.

PAINTED TURTLE
Chrysemys picta   ALL NORTHEAST STATES

Where: Almost any type of freshwater wetland that has some sun exposure; rarely also in brackish wetlands.

Tips: Look for them basking in sun on partially submerged logs, rocks and other exposed features on sunny, warm days.

- **Adult size:** ~4.5-7 in. long.
- **Clutch details:** Female typically deposits 5-6 eggs underground in a nest that she excavates; sometimes have 2 clutches in a year.
- Named for ornate color patterns around the edge of their top shell (the "carapace"), their bottom shell (the "plastron"), and striped patterns along their legs, neck, head, and tail.
- The most widely distributed turtle species in the U.S., currently present in all lower 48 U.S. States except for Colorado and Nevada; although the populations in California and Florida are the result of human introductions.
- Males perform a mating "dance" to entice a female, which includes facing the female and waving his long front claws.
- Like most turtles, the sex of the young developing in eggs is determined entirely by the temperature of the eggs when in the nest; colder temperatures lead to more males and warmer temperatures result in more females. This is known as "Temperature Dependent Sex Determination".
- Typically overwinter in mud or decaying vegetation at the bottom of wetlands; are one of the earliest turtles to emerge, doing so in late-Winter to early-Spring.
- While basking in the sun is primarily to warm themselves up, often it has the added advantage helping rid them of leeches.

Spotted Turtle

Clemmys guttata   All Northeast States

Where: Typically found in small and shallow wetlands such as shrub swamps, marshes, wet meadows, beaver ponds, ditches, bogs, and others.

Tips: One of the most likely turtle species to find in vernal pools.

- **Adult size:** ~4-5 in. long; the 2nd smallest turtle species in the Northeast. The Bog Turtle, a federally-threatened species, is the smallest native turtle species in the Northeast.

- **Clutch details:** Female typically deposits 3-4 eggs underground in a nest she excavates; among the fewest eggs per clutch of all native turtle species in the Northeast.

- Named for the yellow spots that they have on the top portion of their shell as well as on their head, neck, and legs which may exceed 100 total spots in some adults.

- One of the earliest active turtles in any given year, often beginning their surface activity as early as March, including sometimes being seen swimming under the ice in late-Winter/early-Spring.

- Travel longer distances in terrestrial environments in a given year than most other aquatic turtles in the Northeast, which occurs during movements to find food as well as to find mates.

- Very sensitive to poor water quality and contamination.

- Often overwinter in, or near the edge of, wetlands under tree or shrub roots or under grass/sedge hummocks.

- Currently listed as a protected species in most States of the Northeast. Illegal collection for the pet trade is one of the biggest threats to their populations in the region.

Snapping Turtle

Chelydra serpentina　　　ALL NORTHEAST STATES

Where: Wide variety of wetlands ranging from lakes, ponds, bogs, swamps, and rivers, among others; mainly those that contain water year-round.

Tips: Watch out for females crossing roads, especially May – June during nesting trips.

- **Adult size:** ~8-17 in. long; often 15-30 lbs., sometimes up to 50+ lbs. The largest freshwater turtle in the Northeast.

- **Clutch details:** Female typically deposits ~25-40 eggs underground in a nest that she excavates; often will travel a far distance from water to lay eggs, including sometimes in vegetable gardens due to these being easy soils to dig in.

- As with all turtle species, Snapping Turtles don't have teeth; they do, however, have a strong, bony, beak-like mouth and jaws with a very powerful bite force that they capture prey with.

- Named for the extremely quick and powerful combined head/neck thrust with biting motion that they make when lunging at prey in the water or to defend themselves when approached by potential predators while on land.

- Eat a wide variety of food items; basically anything they can fit in their mouth, from a wide variety of fish, amphibians, small mammals, and birds as well as a large amount of vegetation.

- Typically reach maturity between 15-20 years old; rarely can live upwards of 100 years in the wild.

- Overwinter at the bottom of wetlands, sometimes under logs or other debris on the bottom.

- As long as you are not harassing them, you don't have to worry about being bitten by a Snapping Turtle when in the water.

Wood Turtle

Glyptemys insculpta   ALL NORTHEAST STATES

Where: In and around slow-moving streams, brooks, and rivers; feed and nest in the surrounding terrestrial areas.

Tips: If you see a Wood Turtle, try to take a photo from a distance and report the specific location to your State's wildlife agency, as this is a rare species.

- **Adult size:** ~5-8 in. long.

- **Clutch details:** Female typically deposits ~4-12 eggs in a nest that she excavates in the uplands surrounding streams, brooks, and rivers; often in locations exposed to ample sunlight such as meadows and powerline rights-of-way.

- Shell on the underside of their body (the "plastron") is yellow with black markings; the pattern of these markings is unique to each individual.

- Lure earthworms (one of their preferred food items) to the surface of the ground by stomping their front feet on the ground. While it is not entirely clear why earthworms come to the surface in response to this, some people use a similar technique to lure worms to the surface to collect for fishing bait.

- Overwinter underwater, typically in undercut stream/riverbanks within exposed roots, or alternatively on the bottoms of the streams/brooks/rivers; most breeding takes place in the water.

- Can live upwards of 80 years and it often takes them 10+ years to reach sexual maturity in the Northeast.

- Previously quite common throughout the Northeast, their populations have declined substantially since the 1970s due primarily to habitat loss and degradation of stream habitats.

- One of the biggest conservation threats are injuries and mortality sustained from agricultural mowing equipment.

Common Gartersnake

Thamnophis sirtalis   ALL NORTHEAST STATES

Where: Found in almost any setting, ranging from fields, meadows, yards, parks, shrublands, forests, wetlands, etc.

Tips: Commonly encountered in yards and gardens, and around sheds and barns.

- **Adult size:** ~18-32 in. long.

- **Clutch details:** Female gives birth to live young; typically between 15-40 young.

- Named for the resemblance of their striped pattern to sock garters; are often referred to as "garden snakes" by people.

- Have a wide diversity of body pattern variations, including variability in the color of stripes and the presence/absence and amount of checkerboard-like patterning throughout their body.

- As noted above, they give birth to live young (known as "viviparity"). Some advantages of giving birth to live young, compared to the young hatching from eggs in a nest, include: 1) the developing young are safer from predators prior to emergence, and 2) the female can bask in the sun to raise her body temperature, which speeds up development of the young.

- Eat almost any animal that is small enough to fit in their mouth, including, among others, a wide range of invertebrates, amphibians, small fish, small rodents, and even other snakes.

- Are more cold-resistant than other snakes in the Northeast and, as such, tend to be active earlier in the Spring and later in the Fall than other snake species.

- Hibernate together with other snakes in a "communal den", which sometimes can comprise hundreds of individual snakes, sometimes including a mix of snake species.

Northern Ring-Necked Snake

Diadophis punctatus   All Northeast States

Where: Typically found in woodlands under debris/cover such as rocks, logs, and similar such objects. Also can be found in more open habitat settings.

Tips: Under large, flat debris (like plywood) on the ground is your best place to find one.

- **Adult size:** ~9-15 in. long; one of the smallest snake species in the Northeast.

- **Clutch details:** Female typically deposits ~2-5 eggs under rocks, logs, or similar such objects and sometimes will lay their eggs in the same location as other Northern Ring-Necked Snakes.

- Named for golden ring around neck; are black above (with faint blueish-gray hue) and bright yellow to yellowish-orange below.

- Will sometimes flip-over the latter ~1/3rd of their body to show the bright coloration in an attempt to scare-off/deter predators.

- Primarily eat small salamanders (such as Eastern Red-Backed Salamanders) as well as earthworms; also eat a variety of insects and smaller snakes such as the Northern Red-Bellied Snake.

- Have weak venom in their saliva to subdue prey, but are completely harmless to humans.

- Active primarily at night, which is atypical of most snake species in the Northeast.

- Though rarely seen, can often be present in very high densities; likely the most populous snake in the Northeast.

- Sometimes will find their way into homes and buildings; likely simply the result of exploring their surrounding environment and in doing so finding their way into small gaps underneath doorways, gaps in basement windows, and cracks in home foundations, for example, given their small size.

Eastern Milksnake

Lampropeltis triangulum   ALL NORTHEAST STATES

Where: Found in a wide range of habitat settings; essentially wherever there are rodent populations.

Tips: Look for them under wide items, such as pieces of plywood, that are laying flat on the ground. Very rarely encountered otherwise.

- **Adult size:** ~24-36 in. long.

- **Clutch details:** Females typically deposit ~6-24 eggs in debris/soil piles or under almost any type of cover object including logs, scrap wood, tarps, etc.

- Named "milk" snake because they are often found in and around barns (due to the abundance of mice and other small mammals in barns) and there was a false belief that they sucked milk from cows at night.

- Primarily eat mice, voles, and other rodents; also eat birds, bird eggs, other snakes, and snake eggs.

- Constrict their prey and then eat them whole. Prey constriction among snake species present in the Northeast is quite uncommon; most eat prey while it is alive.

- Active primarily at night, which is atypical of most snake species in the Northeast; nighttime is when their main prey items (mice and other small rodents) are the most active.

- Overwinter together underground, in a state of reduced metabolic activity called "brumation" (analogous to torpor or hibernation that many mammals undergo); typically in deep rock crevices with other snakes, including other snake species.

- Sometimes mis-identified as Copperheads due to their somewhat similar body patterning and coloration, and are sometimes intentionally killed by humans as a result.

Eastern Hognose Snake

Heterodon platirhinos   CT, MA, NH, RI

Where: Open habitats such as shrublands, dunes, and sparse forest, and that have sandy soil.

Tips: Rarely encountered due to being well-camouflaged and having a limited distribution. Under wide items laying on the ground (like plywood) is your best chance to see one.

- **Adult size:** ~20-40 in. long.
- **Clutch details:** Female deposits ~6-30 eggs in sandy soil and/or under some cover object.
- Named "hognose" snake due to their upturned snout; they use this primarily to dig up toads burrowed into/under the ground.
- Other adaptations for eating toads (their primary prey) include:
    - oversized adrenal glands that release chemicals which counteract toad toxins
    - fangs in the back of their mouth that they use to deflate toads which have puffed themselves with air to try to make themselves too big to eat
    - a mild toxin that they inject in prey to subdue them (this does not pose a risk/threat to humans or to pets)
- When they feel threatened they often will exhibit some or all of these following behaviors:
    - inflate their bodies and hiss to try to scare the predator away
    - raise their head, flatten their "hood" *(see photo above)*, and strike their head (with mouth closed) towards the predator
    - flip upside-down and play dead, including regurgitating any food in their digestive system and emitting a musky smelling secretion to make themself less palatable; when playing dead will hang their tongue out the side of their mouth and will flip themself back upside-down if you flip them rightside-up

COMMON WATERSNAKE
Nerodia sipedon   ALL NORTHEAST STATES

Where: Spend most of their time in, and nearby, a wide variety of wetland types.

Tips: Look for them basking in the sun atop logs, rocks, and tussocks of grasses in wetlands nearby shore, particularly on warm days during Spring.

- **Adult size:** ~24-42 in. long.
- **Clutch details:** Female gives birth to ~20-40 live young.
- Also well-known as the "Northern Watersnake".
- Primarily eat fish and amphibians; also eat crayfish, insects, and small mammals. Are known to herd schools of small fish and tadpoles towards shore to capture many at a time.
- Are great swimmers and can capture prey both underwater and above-water on land, exposed vegetation, logs, etc.
- Able to stay underwater during the active season for more than an hour at a time, though typically only do so when they feel threatened by a potential predator.
- Most active during the daytime, but also, not infrequently, are active at night, including for hunting purposes.
- Overwinter either underwater, in beaver lodges, or underground in crevices, mammal burrows, or holes near the edge of wetlands; often overwinter as a group of multiple individuals together, sometimes with other snake species.
- Are not poisonous; sometimes mis-identified as Cottonmouths due to their somewhat similar physical appearance, habitats used, and their behavioral habits. Are intentionally killed by humans sometimes as a result of this mis-identification. Cottonmouths are not found north of Virginia.

How You Can Help Wildlife

Below is a list of different things you can do to help wildlife; the pages that follow provide more detail on each.

At Home:
- Plant pollinator-friendly garden(s)/meadow(s)
- Don't use herbicides or pesticides on your lawn or garden
- Participate in "No Mow May"
- Allow at least 2-3 weeks between lawn-mowings
- Consider putting out bee baths
- Retain leaf litter in your gardens over the Winter
- Provide good habitat diversity in your yard
- Turn-off outdoor lights at night when not in use
- Secure outdoor garbage cans, compost bins, and livestock food containers
- Don't allow your cat(s) to roam free outdoors
- If you feed birds, make sure to follow responsible bird-feeding practices
- Consider having a bird bath(s)
- Affix window decals to reduce bird strikes

On the Road:
- Minimize your driving on warm, rainy Spring/Summer nights to reduce amphibian road-kill
- Never throw food products out your vehicle window

Out and About:
- Don't feed wildlife
- Clean-up trash you come across while outside

General:
- Share your knowledge about, and passion for, wildlife with others
- Support wildlife conservation and land conservation organizations
- Volunteer

How You Can Help Wildlife

- **Plant pollinator-friendly garden(s)/meadow(s)**

  - **Why**: These provide critical food sources for a wide diversity of pollinators and seed-eating birds and mammals, as well as habitat for many species.

  - Ideally plant with native species, as many pollinator species have co-evolved with local, native plant species.

  - Visit a local plant nursery for advice on good options of species to seed/plant and when to do so.

  - If you don't have space for a garden or meadow, or don't want to do that much, raised plant beds or even just pots planted with wildflowers can be helpful for pollinators.

- **Don't use herbicides or pesticides on your lawn or garden**

  - **Why**: Beyond the many and varied risks to human health, herbicides and pesticides often have significant, negative impacts on a wide variety of wildlife; this includes disrupting their hormones which impacts their behavior and ability to reproduce, and can kill them. Also, pesticides reduce available invertebrate food for a variety of birds and bats.

  - Visit a local plant nursery, and/or search online, to find alternative and safer ways to deal with unwanted "pests".

    - For example, planting garlic in and amongst your vegetables will help repel Japanese Beetles, weevils, aphids and mites; basil planted next to tomato plants will have a similar repellant effect on horn worms.

How You Can Help Wildlife

- **Participate in "No Mow May"**

    - **Why**: By waiting at least until June to first mow your lawn each year, this allows small, early-season wildflowers (such as violets) to flower which are critical early-season nectar sources for bumblebees emerging from hibernation.

    - You can buy a sign online, or make one yourself, to put in your front yard to spread the word and to inform your neighbors why you are not mowing your lawn.

- **Allow at least 2-3 weeks between lawn-mowings**

    - **Why**: If you do mow your lawn, doing so less frequently throughout the growing-season allows small wildflowers to bloom in between mowing sessions, which can be important sources of nectar for a wide variety of pollinators.

- **Consider putting out bee baths**

    - **Why**: Bee baths provide a reliable source of water for bees for drinking, to bring back to their hive to help keep the hive cool, and to bring back for their young.

    - Look online for best practices; here are some :

- Use a shallow dish; preferably glass or ceramic, as plastics may leach into the water.

- Place dish slightly perched (such as atop an upside-down flower pot) in shade near flowers or your garden.

- Place stones in the bee bath so that bees can stand on them to stay dry while they are drinking.

- Replace with fresh water daily.

How You Can Help Wildlife

- **Retain leaf litter in your gardens over the Winter**
  - **Why**: This provides critical cover and insulation for bumblebees and other pollinators that overwinter in loose soil and/or in leaf litter. Additionally, many birds present in Winter in the region feed on invertebrates found in leaf litter.

  - An added bonus to this is that decomposing leaves add nutrients to the soil which have other beneficial advantages for plant growth as a natural fertilizer source.

- **Provide good habitat diversity in your yard**
  - **Why**: This increases the number of species that can benefit from your yard and the different types of benefits (such as for food, nesting, overwintering, etc.) that your yard can provide for different species.

  - Plant a range of native shrub species. Visit a local plant nursery for advice about species to plant given your yard's growing conditions and related to the types of species and habitat attributes (e.g., berries for migrating birds, bird nesting habitat, nectar for pollinators, etc.) you want to provide for.

  - Create debris piles using fallen branches and other woody debris; this provides cover from predators, feeding habitat for some birds, and nesting habitat for a range of species.

  - Where safe, leave standing dead trees as these are used by a wide-variety of bird and mammal species for nesting cavities.

How You Can Help Wildlife

- **Turn-off outdoor lights at night when not in use**
  - **Why**: Artificial nighttime lights, among other impacts:
    - negatively impact bird migrations
    - draw in moths and other types of invertebrates which are then more easily found and eaten by predators
    - lead to reduced feeding by small mammals due to increased risk of exposure to predators
    - result in a reduction in resting time and resting quality for a large number of species
  - If there are lights that you need to keep on at night, consider:
    - replacing them with downward-facing lights and/or affixing shields above and around the light to reduce unnecessary upward and/or outward spread of light
    - replacing them with lights located closer to the ground
    - using a lower-lumens bulb
    - using bulbs with amber or red bulbs, which appear dimmer to many species
    - putting the light(s) on a timer so that they are only on when necessary

- **Secure outdoor garbage cans, compost bins, and livestock food containers**
  - **Why**: This reduces the risk of wildlife such as Black Bears, Raccoons, Skunks, and other species from being attracted to these unnatural sources of food.
  - Animals can get sick or die from eating specific types of foods and/or moldy foods, get intestinal blockages, get injured eating and/or handling glass and plastic shards, etc.
  - Animals, such as Black Bears, can become more active during the dormant season where they can readily access unnatural food sources, which can have a variety of negative effects.

How You Can Help Wildlife

- **Don't allow your cat(s) to roam free outdoors**
    - **Why**: Cats are incredibly skilled predators and cats allowed to range freely outdoors kill huge numbers of animals including birds, mammals, amphibians, reptiles, and invertebrates.
    - A study published in 2014 estimated that free-ranging domestic cats kill between 1.3-4.0 billion birds and between 6.3-22.3 billion mammals each year in the U.S.
    - One in-between alternative is to provide your cat(s) access to the outdoors via a wildlife-safe "catio" (a wire-mesh based enclosure that your cat(s) can access via a cat-door from a window or door of your home); this has the additional advantage of being a safer outdoor option for your cat(s).

- **If you feed birds, make sure to follow responsible bird-feeding practices**
    - **Why**: Backyard bird-feeding can help supplement natural food availability which has declined as a result of human development, herbicide/pesticide use, etc. However, this can alter bird behavior and concentrate them in high densities.
    - Look online for best practices; here are some:
        - During the period of the year in which you feed birds, keep your feeders stocked with seed/feed at all times.
        - Keep feeders a good distance from your home to reduce the risk of window strikes by birds.
        - Clean feeders biweekly to prevent spread of disease.
        - Take your bird feeders down permanently if they have been visited by bears, as bears have a great memory of where they have accessed easy food sources in the past.

How You Can Help Wildlife

- **Consider having a bird bath(s)**

  - **Why**: Bird baths provide a reliable source of water for birds for the purposes of drinking and for bathing.

  - Look online for best practices; here are some :

    - Get a bird bath with a gentle slope so birds can wade in it.

    - Keep water depth at ~0.5-1 inch at the edge and ~2 inches in the middle. Replace the water every day or two.

    - Place stones in the bird bath so that birds can stand on them to stay dry when drinking.

- **Affix window decals to reduce bird strikes**

  - **Why**: It is estimated that ~1 billion birds strike glass windows each year in the U.S., as they don't realize they are a barrier; they sometimes get confused and see a reflection of the sky, see plants inside, etc. and are attracted to windows as a result.

  - There are a wide variety of window decals you can purchase online that are effective in reducing window strikes by birds.

- **Minimize your driving on warm, rainy Spring nights to reduce amphibian road-kill**

  - **Why**: Though difficult to estimate, hundreds of millions, or more, of amphibians are run-over by vehicles each year in the U.S. when crossing roads during their seasonal migrations.

  - Most amphibian migrations take place during warm, rainy Spring nights, so reducing or eliminating driving during those conditions will reduce the amount of road-kill that occurs.

  - If you drive during these conditions, stay off of rural/back-roads as these are ones with the most amphibians.

How You Can Help Wildlife

- **Never throw food products our your vehicle window**
  - **Why**: Food and food scraps attract wildlife, and anything that attracts wildlife closer to roads increases their risk of being hit and killed by vehicles.
  - Throwing apple cores, banana peels, etc. out a vehicle's window, while many may not view as littering and/or harmful, has the negative effect of bringing wildlife closer to roads.

- **Don't feed wildlife**
  - **Why**: Feeding wildlife negatively impacts wild animals in a variety of different ways and thus is something that you shouldn't do; backyard birdfeeders are a partial exception to this *(see discussion on backyard bird-feeding on page 116)*.
  - Some consequences include:
    - Habituating wild individuals to humans.
    - Bringing individuals in close proximity to one another, which increases the risk of spreading disease.

    - Attracting predators, therefore increasing the likelihood that the fed animals are killed by predators.
    - Causing malnourishment (for example, feeding ducks bread fills them up but lacks many essential nutrients that they otherwise would get by eating natural food sources).

- **Clean-up trash you come across while outside**
  - **Why**: Ingestion of litter can have a variety of negative effects on wildlife *(see discussion of this on page 115)*; also, wildlife can be severely injured or killed by becoming entangled in litter such as fishing line, plastic bags, bottles, etc.
    - For example, many Ospreys have been killed in entanglements with discarded fishing line *(see page 22)*.

How You Can Help Wildlife

- **Share your knowledge about, and passion for, wildlife with others**
  - **Why**: The more that people know about wildlife, the more connected they will feel to them and thus will be more likely to do things, and support efforts, to help conserve them.
  - In addition to sharing directly with others, you can also use social media postings to share your wildlife- and nature-related photos, experiences, knowledge, etc.

- **Support wildlife conservation and land conservation organizations**
  - **Why**: It is in large part due to the work of these organizations that we still have a number of species and critical habitats that otherwise likely would not still exist due to impacts of human development and activities on the natural environment.
  - Many of these organizations, especially those that are local/private, are largely-, if not entirely-, dependent on private donations in order to fund their work.
  - You can be creative in this fundraising including doing a 5k or a walk-a-thon, start a social media fundraising campaign, have a yard sale, etc. These can have the added benefit of building community support for these organizations.

- **Volunteer**
  - **Why**: Many wildlife and environmental organizations have limited funding and thus rely heavily on volunteers to do a good amount of the work that they do.
  - You can help doing trail work, invasive plant removal, organizing, fundraising, education, and in many other ways; find an organization you want to help and ask them how you can help.

WILDLIFE-RELATED ACTIVITIES

Below are some (of many possible) wildlife-related activities that you can do by yourself and/or with others.

- **Keep a list** of the different wildlife species that you find in your yard, around your neighborhood, at your favorite park, etc.
    - You can use the checklist appendices in this book to do so, and you can even keep track of the month(s) in which you've seen each species.
- **Download free smartphone apps** which help you identify animals and plants from photos, birds from their songs, etc. You can submit your observations, which can be valuable data for the scientific community. Some great apps are:
    - *iNaturalist*: animal and plant identification from photos that you take
    - *Seek*: an alternative iNaturalist app for animal and plant identification by pointing your smartphone camera at the animal/plant (you don't have to take a photo)
    - *Merlin*: bird species identification from their song

- **Visit** different parks, wildlife sanctuaries, conservation areas, and other types of natural areas to explore the diversity of habitats and species that they contain.
- **Join a guided nature walk** (for example at a local Audubon sanctuary, at a local conservation area, or at an urban park) to learn more about the nature nearby where you live.
- **Keep a nature journal** to keep a record of your observations, outings, drawings of animals/plants/landscapes, and more.
- **Practice your identification of animal tracks** by going out in Winter to try to identify tracks you find in the snow; you can do the same thing during any time of the year in muddy spots as well.

WILDLIFE-RELATED ACTIVITIES

- **Try to find as many cavities in trees** in your yard, neighborhood, favorite park, etc. and keep track of different species that you see using cavities.

- **See how many Gray Squirrel nests** you can find in the trees in your yard, around your neighborhood, at your favorite park, etc. Then watch those nests to see which ones actively have squirrels using them.

- **Look for Monarch Butterfly caterpillars and chrysalids** on milkweed plants in late-Summer into early-Fall.

- **Try to identify the bird species mimicked** by Northern Mockingbirds or Gray Catbirds when they are singing.

- **Build or buy a birdhouse** and put it up in your yard; then keep an eye on it to watch for birds nesting in it.

- **Participate in "FeederWatch"** if you have bird feeders. This is important information you can contribute to the scientific community. Go to https://feederwatch.org to learn more.

- **Set-up a trail camera** in your yard and see what animals you catch on it. You might be surprised at species that use your yard at night that you might not have been aware of. You can set one up facing your bird bath, if you have one, and get some great pictures and videos from that.

- **Conduct a backyard moth survey** at night with a white sheet fully stretched-out and hung from a tree-branch or clothes-line and and back-lit by a black light. You can use the iNaturalist smartphone app to help identify the different moths you see. You will be very surprised how many different types you see.

Glossary

The definitions below have been composed with reference to their application to wildlife and, as such, have not been extracted from any formal dictionary.

anting: a behavior documented in more than 200 bird species whereby they rub and/or place a large number of ants on their body and feathers to use the formic acid in ants to remove parasites and/or to soothe their skin after feather replacement.

brackish: water with salt in it, but not as high of a concentration of salt as ocean saltwater (which is ~35 parts per million).

broken-wing display: a behavior exhibited by a number of bird species whereby a parent bird pretends to have a broken-wing as it then moves away from the location of its nest as a way to lure a predator away from the nest.

brood *(noun)* : a group of young from a given nesting/breeding event; most commonly used when describing the young birds that were hatched from a nest of eggs.

brood parasitism: when one species has another species raise its young, typically to the detriment of the young of the host species; Brown-Headed Cowbird *(page 56)* is a classic example of this.

brumation: an extended period of inactivity and reduced metabolic activity exhibited by reptiles, typically during cold seasons and/or lengthy cold spells; similar to "torpor" exhibited by some mammals.

cache *(noun)* : an accumulated storage of food to consume at a later day/time. *(verb)* : the act of storing/hiding away food for later consumption; this is common among a variety of wildlife species for the purposes of having food sources during Winter.

carapace: the top shell of a turtle.

carotenoids: a group of pigments in many plants that are responsible for bright yellow, orange, and red coloration in different parts of the plant including the fruit; many birds get at least some of their bright coloration from eating fruits from these plants that have high carotenoid concentrations.

Glossary

cavity-nesting: a behavior whereby animals (primarily many bird and mammal species) nest in a sheltered chamber (or "cavity"); typical examples include cavities in the sides of trees, burrows in earthen banks, and crevices in rock faces.

clutch *(noun)* : a group of eggs from a nesting/breeding event.

coprophagia: a behavior whereby animals eat their own defecation to maximize nutrient intake.

courtship display: behaviors that animals perform to attract a member of the opposite sex for mating purposes.

crepuscular: active during dawn and dusk.

crest *(noun)* : a group of longer, and often more flexible, feathers atop the head of some birds, the height of which can be modified at any given time as a way to non-verbally communicate with other birds (for example, to communicate aggression).

crop *(noun)* : an expanded, pouch-like portion of the esophagus, found in some bird species (though is also present in some insects), primarily used as a temporary storage place for food prior to digestion, though also can be used to store a milk-like liquid in doves and pigeons that they feed to their young.

diurnal: active during the daytime.

drumming: a behavior most frequently exhibited by woodpeckers where they use loud drilling with their bill against trees and other hard surfaces to communicate to other birds; mainly to attract mates and to define their territory to other individuals.

echolocation: the way bats (and some other animals such as dolphins, whales, and others) find their prey; this works in bats whereby they emit high frequency sound pulses from their mouth or nose and then, by listening to the returning echo, they are able to pinpoint the location and size of the prey item(s).

ectotherm: animals that rely on external sources (such as sunlight and ambient environmental temperatures) to regulate their body temperature; colloquially referred to as "cold-blooded" animals.

Glossary

foraging: a synonym of "feeding".

home range: the area over which an individual lives and moves on a regular basis .

mange: a skin disease of non-human mammals caused by an infestation of parasitic mites that burrow into the skin and/or hair follicles, often leads to intense itching, hair loss, and can be fatal.

marsupial: a group of mammal species wherein the young are born not fully developed and typically complete their development in a pouch in the abdominal area of the mother within which they suckle while they complete their development.

midden: a stash of food collected by squirrels; typically at the base of conifer trees, often comprised mainly of scales of cones within which cones are stored.

mobbing: an anti-predator behavior whereby multiple individuals of a prey species harass a predator as a group as a way to move the predator out of the area, typically as a means of protecting young. This is most often seen in birds, where smaller birds, of different species, will cooperatively mob a hawk or owl.

nictitating membrane: a translucent membrane, found in a wide range of animals, that is functionally an inner eyelid which protects the eyes so that the animal can see underwater and also to keep them moist and free from dust in other situations.

nocturnal: active at night.

pellet: undigested parts of food, often primarily bony material, that are regurgitated as a mass by an animal; these parts tend to be too dangerous to be passed through the digestive tract; most common in owls, though exhibited by other bird species as well.

plastron: the bottom shell of a turtle.

plumage: all of the feathers of an individual bird.

plumes: special types of feathers in some birds that are used for ornamental purposes, typically for attracting a mate(s).

Glossary

prehensile: describing something that is designed/adapted for grasping, especially by wrapping around; such as describing the ability of some mammals (for example, the Virginia Opossum) to use their tail for holding on to branches with.

raptor: predatory birds; including hawks, falcons, kites, eagles, vultures, and owls.

roost: *(noun):* a location where birds rest and sleep; often up in trees and sometimes in communal groups such as is exhibited by crows during the non-breeding season. *(verb)* : to congregate or to settle, typically for rest and sleep (related to birds and bats).

scat: another word for defecation.

sentry: an individual, typically within a group of animals feeding (often with respect to birds), that looks out for potential predators while the rest of the individuals in the group feed.

siblicide: a behavior, mainly exhibited in birds compared to other animals, whereby a young offspring of a brood/litter will kill one or more of its siblings to ensure itself maximal food resources; most frequently occurs in situations wherein food is scarce.

snag: a dead tree (entire, or part thereof) that is still standing.

syrinx: the vocal organ of birds.

thermals: columns of rising air created by warming of the earth's surface (including water, ground, paved and/or other such artificial surfaces) that many birds glide on to travel and/or hover with limited, to sometime no, use of wing-flapping.

torpor: a state of dormancy and reduced metabolic activity experienced by some mammal species, typically during cold seasons; similar to "brumation" of reptiles.

tympanum: an external hearing structure, somewhat analogous to the eardrum, that is present in a number of types of animals; most frequently referred to in the context of many frog species.

References and Related Readings

Information contained in this book was primarily compiled from the author's professional experience and education, via consultation and collaboration with colleagues, and from a variety of reliable sources which are a subset of those below.

Alden, P., and B. Cassie. 1998. National Audubon Society Field Guide to New England: Connecticut, Maine, Massachusetts, New Hampshire, Rhode Island, Vermont. Knopf Publishing.

American Bird Conservancy. ABC's Bird Library. https://abcbirds.org/birds.

Audubon Society. Guide to North American Birds. https://audubon.org/field-guide/bird.

Connecticut Department of Energy & Environmental Protection. Wildlife Fact Sheets. https://portal.ct.gov/DEEP/Wildlife/Learn-About-Wildlife/Wildlife-Fact-Sheets.

Cornell Lab of Ornithology. All About Birds. Cornell Lab of Ornithology, Ithaca, New York. https://www.allaboutbirds.org.

DeGraaf, R.M., and D.D. Rudis. 1986. New England Wildlife: Habitat, Natural History, and Distribution. Gen. Tech. Rep. NE-108. Broomall, PA: U.S. Department of Agriculture, Forest Service, Northeastern Forest Experimental Station. https://doi.org/10.2737/NE-GTR-108.

Hunter Jr., M.L., A.J.K. Calhoun, and M. McCollough. 1999. Maine Amphibians and Reptiles. The University of Maine Press.

Kaufman, K., and K. Kaufman. 2012. Kaufman Field Guide to Nature of New England. Houghton Mifflin Harcourt Co.

Kenney, L.P., and M.R. Burne. 2009. A Field Guide to the Animals of Vernal Pools. Massachusetts Division of Fisheries & Wildlife.

Klemens, M.W. 1993. Amphibians and Reptiles of Connecticut and Adjacent Regions. Connecticut Department of Energy and Environmental Protection.

References and Related Readings

Klemens, M.W., H.J. Gruner, D.P. Quinn, and E.R. Davison. 2021. Conservation of Amphibians and Reptiles in Connecticut. Connecticut Department of Energy and Environmental Protection.

Maine Department of Inland Fisheries & Wildlife. Wildlife Species Information. https://www.maine.gov/ifw/fish-wildlife/wildlife/species-information.

Marchand, P.J. 2010. Nature Guide to the Northern Forest: Exploring the Ecology of the Forests of New York, New Hampshire, Vermont, and Maine. Appalachian Mountain Club Books.

Massachusetts Audubon Society. Nature & Wildlife. https://www.massaudubon.org/learn/nature-wildlife.

Massachusetts Division of Fisheries and Wildlife. Massachusetts Wildlife Library. https://www.mass.gov/lists/massachusetts-wildlife-library.

Myers, P., R. Espinosa, C.S. Parr, T. Jones, G.S. Hammond, and T.A. Dewey. The Animal Diversity Web (online). https://animaldiversity.org.

New Hampshire Fish and Game. Species Occurring in New Hampshire. https://www.wildlife.state.nh.us/wildlife/species-list.html.

New York State Department of Environmental Conservation. Animals, Plants, Aquatic Life. https://www.dec.ny.gov/23.html.

Vermont Fish & Wildlife Department. Vermont Critters. https://vtfishandwildlife.com/learn-more/vermont-critters.

Bird Species Checklist

Here you can keep track of all of the bird species in this book you've seen and the month(s) you've seen each in.

Lines have been added to make it easier to navigate the grid

Waterbirds

	Jan	Feb	Mar	Apr	May	Jun	Jul	Aug	Sep	Oct	Nov	Dec
☐ Belted Kingfisher	☐	☐	☐	☐	☐	☐	☐	☐	☐	☐	☐	☐
☐ Great Blue Heron	☐	☐	☐	☐	☐	☐	☐	☐	☐	☐	☐	☐
☐ Great Egret	☐	☐	☐	☐	☐	☐	☐	☐	☐	☐	☐	☐
☐ Common Loon	☐	☐	☐	☐	☐	☐	☐	☐	☐	☐	☐	☐
☐ Double-Crested Cormorant	☐	☐	☐	☐	☐	☐	☐	☐	☐	☐	☐	☐
☐ Canada Goose	☐	☐	☐	☐	☐	☐	☐	☐	☐	☐	☐	☐
☐ Mute Swan	☐	☐	☐	☐	☐	☐	☐	☐	☐	☐	☐	☐
☐ Wood Duck	☐	☐	☐	☐	☐	☐	☐	☐	☐	☐	☐	☐
☐ Mallard	☐	☐	☐	☐	☐	☐	☐	☐	☐	☐	☐	☐
☐ Common Merganser	☐	☐	☐	☐	☐	☐	☐	☐	☐	☐	☐	☐
☐ Hooded Merganser	☐	☐	☐	☐	☐	☐	☐	☐	☐	☐	☐	☐

Gulls

	Jan	Feb	Mar	Apr	May	Jun	Jul	Aug	Sep	Oct	Nov	Dec
☐ Herring Gull	☐	☐	☐	☐	☐	☐	☐	☐	☐	☐	☐	☐
☐ Ring-Billed Gull	☐	☐	☐	☐	☐	☐	☐	☐	☐	☐	☐	☐

Raptors

	Jan	Feb	Mar	Apr	May	Jun	Jul	Aug	Sep	Oct	Nov	Dec
☐ Turkey Vulture	☐	☐	☐	☐	☐	☐	☐	☐	☐	☐	☐	☐
☐ Osprey	☐	☐	☐	☐	☐	☐	☐	☐	☐	☐	☐	☐
☐ Bald Eagle	☐	☐	☐	☐	☐	☐	☐	☐	☐	☐	☐	☐
☐ Red-Tailed Hawk	☐	☐	☐	☐	☐	☐	☐	☐	☐	☐	☐	☐
☐ Cooper's Hawk	☐	☐	☐	☐	☐	☐	☐	☐	☐	☐	☐	☐
☐ Peregrine Falcon	☐	☐	☐	☐	☐	☐	☐	☐	☐	☐	☐	☐
☐ American Kestrel	☐	☐	☐	☐	☐	☐	☐	☐	☐	☐	☐	☐
☐ Great Horned Owl	☐	☐	☐	☐	☐	☐	☐	☐	☐	☐	☐	☐
☐ Barred Owl	☐	☐	☐	☐	☐	☐	☐	☐	☐	☐	☐	☐

Backyard Birds	Jan	Feb	Mar	Apr	May	Jun	Jul	Aug	Sep	Oct	Nov	Dec
☐ Ruby-Throated Hummingbird	☐	☐	☐	☐	☐	☐	☐	☐	☐	☐	☐	☐
☐ Downy Woodpecker	☐	☐	☐	☐	☐	☐	☐	☐	☐	☐	☐	☐
☐ Northern Flicker	☐	☐	☐	☐	☐	☐	☐	☐	☐	☐	☐	☐
☐ White-Breasted Nuthatch	☐	☐	☐	☐	☐	☐	☐	☐	☐	☐	☐	☐
☐ Blue Jay	☐	☐	☐	☐	☐	☐	☐	☐	☐	☐	☐	☐
☐ Northern Cardinal	☐	☐	☐	☐	☐	☐	☐	☐	☐	☐	☐	☐
☐ American Robin	☐	☐	☐	☐	☐	☐	☐	☐	☐	☐	☐	☐
☐ Baltimore Oriole	☐	☐	☐	☐	☐	☐	☐	☐	☐	☐	☐	☐
☐ Eastern Bluebird	☐	☐	☐	☐	☐	☐	☐	☐	☐	☐	☐	☐
☐ Mourning Dove	☐	☐	☐	☐	☐	☐	☐	☐	☐	☐	☐	☐
☐ Gray Catbird	☐	☐	☐	☐	☐	☐	☐	☐	☐	☐	☐	☐
☐ Northern Mockingbird	☐	☐	☐	☐	☐	☐	☐	☐	☐	☐	☐	☐
☐ European Starling	☐	☐	☐	☐	☐	☐	☐	☐	☐	☐	☐	☐
☐ Common Grackle	☐	☐	☐	☐	☐	☐	☐	☐	☐	☐	☐	☐
☐ American Crow	☐	☐	☐	☐	☐	☐	☐	☐	☐	☐	☐	☐
☐ Eastern Phoebe	☐	☐	☐	☐	☐	☐	☐	☐	☐	☐	☐	☐
☐ Cedar Waxwing	☐	☐	☐	☐	☐	☐	☐	☐	☐	☐	☐	☐
☐ Tufted Titmouse	☐	☐	☐	☐	☐	☐	☐	☐	☐	☐	☐	☐
☐ Black-Capped Chickadee	☐	☐	☐	☐	☐	☐	☐	☐	☐	☐	☐	☐
☐ American Goldfinch	☐	☐	☐	☐	☐	☐	☐	☐	☐	☐	☐	☐
☐ House Finch	☐	☐	☐	☐	☐	☐	☐	☐	☐	☐	☐	☐
☐ Song Sparrow	☐	☐	☐	☐	☐	☐	☐	☐	☐	☐	☐	☐
☐ House Sparrow	☐	☐	☐	☐	☐	☐	☐	☐	☐	☐	☐	☐
☐ Carolina Wren	☐	☐	☐	☐	☐	☐	☐	☐	☐	☐	☐	☐

Other Birds	Jan	Feb	Mar	Apr	May	Jun	Jul	Aug	Sep	Oct	Nov	Dec
☐ Wild Turkey	☐	☐	☐	☐	☐	☐	☐	☐	☐	☐	☐	☐
☐ Pileated Woodpecker	☐	☐	☐	☐	☐	☐	☐	☐	☐	☐	☐	☐
☐ Brown-Headed Cowbird	☐	☐	☐	☐	☐	☐	☐	☐	☐	☐	☐	☐
☐ Red-Winged Blackbird	☐	☐	☐	☐	☐	☐	☐	☐	☐	☐	☐	☐
☐ Wood Thrush	☐	☐	☐	☐	☐	☐	☐	☐	☐	☐	☐	☐
☐ Ovenbird	☐	☐	☐	☐	☐	☐	☐	☐	☐	☐	☐	☐
☐ Eastern Kingbird	☐	☐	☐	☐	☐	☐	☐	☐	☐	☐	☐	☐
☐ Tree Swallow	☐	☐	☐	☐	☐	☐	☐	☐	☐	☐	☐	☐
☐ Rock Pigeon	☐	☐	☐	☐	☐	☐	☐	☐	☐	☐	☐	☐

Additional Bird Species Checklist

Here you can add, and keep track of, other bird species you've seen that aren't in this book.

		Jan	Feb	Mar	Apr	May	Jun	Jul	Aug	Sep	Oct	Nov	Dec
☐		☐	☐	☐	☐	☐	☐	☐	☐	☐	☐	☐	☐
☐		☐	☐	☐	☐	☐	☐	☐	☐	☐	☐	☐	☐
☐		☐	☐	☐	☐	☐	☐	☐	☐	☐	☐	☐	☐
☐		☐	☐	☐	☐	☐	☐	☐	☐	☐	☐	☐	☐
☐		☐	☐	☐	☐	☐	☐	☐	☐	☐	☐	☐	☐
☐		☐	☐	☐	☐	☐	☐	☐	☐	☐	☐	☐	☐
☐		☐	☐	☐	☐	☐	☐	☐	☐	☐	☐	☐	☐
☐		☐	☐	☐	☐	☐	☐	☐	☐	☐	☐	☐	☐
☐		☐	☐	☐	☐	☐	☐	☐	☐	☐	☐	☐	☐
☐		☐	☐	☐	☐	☐	☐	☐	☐	☐	☐	☐	☐
☐		☐	☐	☐	☐	☐	☐	☐	☐	☐	☐	☐	☐
☐		☐	☐	☐	☐	☐	☐	☐	☐	☐	☐	☐	☐
☐		☐	☐	☐	☐	☐	☐	☐	☐	☐	☐	☐	☐

Additional Bird Species Checklist

Here you can add, and keep track of, other bird species you've seen that aren't in this book.

		JAN	FEB	MAR	APR	MAY	JUN	JUL	AUG	SEP	OCT	NOV	DEC
☐		☐	☐	☐	☐	☐	☐	☐	☐	☐	☐	☐	☐
☐		☐	☐	☐	☐	☐	☐	☐	☐	☐	☐	☐	☐
☐		☐	☐	☐	☐	☐	☐	☐	☐	☐	☐	☐	☐
☐		☐	☐	☐	☐	☐	☐	☐	☐	☐	☐	☐	☐
☐		☐	☐	☐	☐	☐	☐	☐	☐	☐	☐	☐	☐
☐		☐	☐	☐	☐	☐	☐	☐	☐	☐	☐	☐	☐
☐		☐	☐	☐	☐	☐	☐	☐	☐	☐	☐	☐	☐
☐		☐	☐	☐	☐	☐	☐	☐	☐	☐	☐	☐	☐
☐		☐	☐	☐	☐	☐	☐	☐	☐	☐	☐	☐	☐
☐		☐	☐	☐	☐	☐	☐	☐	☐	☐	☐	☐	☐
☐		☐	☐	☐	☐	☐	☐	☐	☐	☐	☐	☐	☐
☐		☐	☐	☐	☐	☐	☐	☐	☐	☐	☐	☐	☐
☐		☐	☐	☐	☐	☐	☐	☐	☐	☐	☐	☐	☐

Additional Bird Species Checklist

Here you can add, and keep track of, other bird species you've seen that aren't in this book.

		Jan	Feb	Mar	Apr	May	Jun	Jul	Aug	Sep	Oct	Nov	Dec
☐		☐	☐	☐	☐	☐	☐	☐	☐	☐	☐	☐	☐
☐		☐	☐	☐	☐	☐	☐	☐	☐	☐	☐	☐	☐
☐		☐	☐	☐	☐	☐	☐	☐	☐	☐	☐	☐	☐
☐		☐	☐	☐	☐	☐	☐	☐	☐	☐	☐	☐	☐
☐		☐	☐	☐	☐	☐	☐	☐	☐	☐	☐	☐	☐
☐		☐	☐	☐	☐	☐	☐	☐	☐	☐	☐	☐	☐
☐		☐	☐	☐	☐	☐	☐	☐	☐	☐	☐	☐	☐
☐		☐	☐	☐	☐	☐	☐	☐	☐	☐	☐	☐	☐
☐		☐	☐	☐	☐	☐	☐	☐	☐	☐	☐	☐	☐
☐		☐	☐	☐	☐	☐	☐	☐	☐	☐	☐	☐	☐
☐		☐	☐	☐	☐	☐	☐	☐	☐	☐	☐	☐	☐
☐		☐	☐	☐	☐	☐	☐	☐	☐	☐	☐	☐	☐
☐		☐	☐	☐	☐	☐	☐	☐	☐	☐	☐	☐	☐

Additional Bird Species Checklist

Here you can add, and keep track of, other bird species you've seen that aren't in this book.

		Jan	Feb	Mar	Apr	May	Jun	Jul	Aug	Sep	Oct	Nov	Dec
☐		☐	☐	☐	☐	☐	☐	☐	☐	☐	☐	☐	☐
☐		☐	☐	☐	☐	☐	☐	☐	☐	☐	☐	☐	☐
☐		☐	☐	☐	☐	☐	☐	☐	☐	☐	☐	☐	☐
☐		☐	☐	☐	☐	☐	☐	☐	☐	☐	☐	☐	☐
☐		☐	☐	☐	☐	☐	☐	☐	☐	☐	☐	☐	☐
☐		☐	☐	☐	☐	☐	☐	☐	☐	☐	☐	☐	☐
☐		☐	☐	☐	☐	☐	☐	☐	☐	☐	☐	☐	☐
☐		☐	☐	☐	☐	☐	☐	☐	☐	☐	☐	☐	☐
☐		☐	☐	☐	☐	☐	☐	☐	☐	☐	☐	☐	☐
☐		☐	☐	☐	☐	☐	☐	☐	☐	☐	☐	☐	☐
☐		☐	☐	☐	☐	☐	☐	☐	☐	☐	☐	☐	☐
☐		☐	☐	☐	☐	☐	☐	☐	☐	☐	☐	☐	☐
☐		☐	☐	☐	☐	☐	☐	☐	☐	☐	☐	☐	☐

Mammal Species Checklist

Here you can keep track of all of the mammal species in this book you've seen and the month(s) you've seen each in.
Lines have been added to make it easier to navigate the grid

Large Mammals	Jan	Feb	Mar	Apr	May	Jun	Jul	Aug	Sep	Oct	Nov	Dec
☐ American Black Bear	☐	☐	☐	☐	☐	☐	☐	☐	☐	☐	☐	☐
☐ Moose	☐	☐	☐	☐	☐	☐	☐	☐	☐	☐	☐	☐
☐ White-Tailed Deer	☐	☐	☐	☐	☐	☐	☐	☐	☐	☐	☐	☐
☐ Eastern Coyote	☐	☐	☐	☐	☐	☐	☐	☐	☐	☐	☐	☐
☐ Bobcat	☐	☐	☐	☐	☐	☐	☐	☐	☐	☐	☐	☐
☐ Red Fox	☐	☐	☐	☐	☐	☐	☐	☐	☐	☐	☐	☐
☐ Gray Fox	☐	☐	☐	☐	☐	☐	☐	☐	☐	☐	☐	☐

Medium-Sized Mammals	Jan	Feb	Mar	Apr	May	Jun	Jul	Aug	Sep	Oct	Nov	Dec
☐ Beaver	☐	☐	☐	☐	☐	☐	☐	☐	☐	☐	☐	☐
☐ North American River Otter	☐	☐	☐	☐	☐	☐	☐	☐	☐	☐	☐	☐
☐ North American Porcupine	☐	☐	☐	☐	☐	☐	☐	☐	☐	☐	☐	☐
☐ Fisher	☐	☐	☐	☐	☐	☐	☐	☐	☐	☐	☐	☐
☐ Long-Tailed Weasel	☐	☐	☐	☐	☐	☐	☐	☐	☐	☐	☐	☐
☐ Woodchuck	☐	☐	☐	☐	☐	☐	☐	☐	☐	☐	☐	☐
☐ Raccoon	☐	☐	☐	☐	☐	☐	☐	☐	☐	☐	☐	☐
☐ Virginia Opossum	☐	☐	☐	☐	☐	☐	☐	☐	☐	☐	☐	☐
☐ Striped Skunk	☐	☐	☐	☐	☐	☐	☐	☐	☐	☐	☐	☐
☐ Eastern Cottontail	☐	☐	☐	☐	☐	☐	☐	☐	☐	☐	☐	☐

Smaller Mammals	Jan	Feb	Mar	Apr	May	Jun	Jul	Aug	Sep	Oct	Nov	Dec
☐ Little Brown Bat	☐	☐	☐	☐	☐	☐	☐	☐	☐	☐	☐	☐
☐ Eastern Gray Squirrel	☐	☐	☐	☐	☐	☐	☐	☐	☐	☐	☐	☐
☐ American Red Squirrel	☐	☐	☐	☐	☐	☐	☐	☐	☐	☐	☐	☐
☐ Northern Flying Squirrel	☐	☐	☐	☐	☐	☐	☐	☐	☐	☐	☐	☐
☐ Eastern Chipmunk	☐	☐	☐	☐	☐	☐	☐	☐	☐	☐	☐	☐
☐ Muskrat	☐	☐	☐	☐	☐	☐	☐	☐	☐	☐	☐	☐
☐ Star-Nosed Mole	☐	☐	☐	☐	☐	☐	☐	☐	☐	☐	☐	☐
☐ Meadow Vole	☐	☐	☐	☐	☐	☐	☐	☐	☐	☐	☐	☐

Additional Mammal Species Checklist

Here you can add, and keep track of, other mammal species you've seen that aren't in this book.

	Species	JAN	FEB	MAR	APR	MAY	JUN	JUL	AUG	SEP	OCT	NOV	DEC
☐		☐	☐	☐	☐	☐	☐	☐	☐	☐	☐	☐	☐
☐		☐	☐	☐	☐	☐	☐	☐	☐	☐	☐	☐	☐
☐		☐	☐	☐	☐	☐	☐	☐	☐	☐	☐	☐	☐
☐		☐	☐	☐	☐	☐	☐	☐	☐	☐	☐	☐	☐
☐		☐	☐	☐	☐	☐	☐	☐	☐	☐	☐	☐	☐
☐		☐	☐	☐	☐	☐	☐	☐	☐	☐	☐	☐	☐
☐		☐	☐	☐	☐	☐	☐	☐	☐	☐	☐	☐	☐
☐		☐	☐	☐	☐	☐	☐	☐	☐	☐	☐	☐	☐
☐		☐	☐	☐	☐	☐	☐	☐	☐	☐	☐	☐	☐
☐		☐	☐	☐	☐	☐	☐	☐	☐	☐	☐	☐	☐
☐		☐	☐	☐	☐	☐	☐	☐	☐	☐	☐	☐	☐
☐		☐	☐	☐	☐	☐	☐	☐	☐	☐	☐	☐	☐
☐		☐	☐	☐	☐	☐	☐	☐	☐	☐	☐	☐	☐

Amphibian & Reptile Species Checklist

Here you can keep track of all of the amphibian & reptile species in this book you've seen and the month(s) you've seen each in.

Lines have been added to make it easier to navigate the grid

Frogs & Toads

	Jan	Feb	Mar	Apr	May	Jun	Jul	Aug	Sep	Oct	Nov	Dec
☐ Wood Frog	☐	☐	☐	☐	☐	☐	☐	☐	☐	☐	☐	☐
☐ American Bullfrog	☐	☐	☐	☐	☐	☐	☐	☐	☐	☐	☐	☐
☐ Spring Peeper	☐	☐	☐	☐	☐	☐	☐	☐	☐	☐	☐	☐
☐ Gray Treefrog	☐	☐	☐	☐	☐	☐	☐	☐	☐	☐	☐	☐
☐ American Toad	☐	☐	☐	☐	☐	☐	☐	☐	☐	☐	☐	☐
☐ Eastern Spadefoot	☐	☐	☐	☐	☐	☐	☐	☐	☐	☐	☐	☐

Salamanders

	Jan	Feb	Mar	Apr	May	Jun	Jul	Aug	Sep	Oct	Nov	Dec
☐ Spotted Salamander	☐	☐	☐	☐	☐	☐	☐	☐	☐	☐	☐	☐
☐ E. Red-Backed Salamander	☐	☐	☐	☐	☐	☐	☐	☐	☐	☐	☐	☐
☐ N. Two-Lined Salamander	☐	☐	☐	☐	☐	☐	☐	☐	☐	☐	☐	☐
☐ Eastern Newt	☐	☐	☐	☐	☐	☐	☐	☐	☐	☐	☐	☐

Turtles

	Jan	Feb	Mar	Apr	May	Jun	Jul	Aug	Sep	Oct	Nov	Dec
☐ Eastern Box Turtle	☐	☐	☐	☐	☐	☐	☐	☐	☐	☐	☐	☐
☐ Painted Turtle	☐	☐	☐	☐	☐	☐	☐	☐	☐	☐	☐	☐
☐ Spotted Turtle	☐	☐	☐	☐	☐	☐	☐	☐	☐	☐	☐	☐
☐ Common Snapping Turtle	☐	☐	☐	☐	☐	☐	☐	☐	☐	☐	☐	☐
☐ Wood Turtle	☐	☐	☐	☐	☐	☐	☐	☐	☐	☐	☐	☐

Snakes

	Jan	Feb	Mar	Apr	May	Jun	Jul	Aug	Sep	Oct	Nov	Dec
☐ Common Gartersnake	☐	☐	☐	☐	☐	☐	☐	☐	☐	☐	☐	☐
☐ Northern Ring-Necked Snake	☐	☐	☐	☐	☐	☐	☐	☐	☐	☐	☐	☐
☐ Eastern Milksnake	☐	☐	☐	☐	☐	☐	☐	☐	☐	☐	☐	☐
☐ Eastern Hognose Snake	☐	☐	☐	☐	☐	☐	☐	☐	☐	☐	☐	☐
☐ Common Watersnake	☐	☐	☐	☐	☐	☐	☐	☐	☐	☐	☐	☐

Additional Amphibian & Reptile Species Checklist

Here you can add, and keep track of other, amphibian and reptile species you've seen that aren't in this book.

		Jan	Feb	Mar	Apr	May	Jun	Jul	Aug	Sep	Oct	Nov	Dec
☐		☐	☐	☐	☐	☐	☐	☐	☐	☐	☐	☐	☐
☐		☐	☐	☐	☐	☐	☐	☐	☐	☐	☐	☐	☐
☐		☐	☐	☐	☐	☐	☐	☐	☐	☐	☐	☐	☐
☐		☐	☐	☐	☐	☐	☐	☐	☐	☐	☐	☐	☐
☐		☐	☐	☐	☐	☐	☐	☐	☐	☐	☐	☐	☐
☐		☐	☐	☐	☐	☐	☐	☐	☐	☐	☐	☐	☐
☐		☐	☐	☐	☐	☐	☐	☐	☐	☐	☐	☐	☐
☐		☐	☐	☐	☐	☐	☐	☐	☐	☐	☐	☐	☐
☐		☐	☐	☐	☐	☐	☐	☐	☐	☐	☐	☐	☐
☐		☐	☐	☐	☐	☐	☐	☐	☐	☐	☐	☐	☐
☐		☐	☐	☐	☐	☐	☐	☐	☐	☐	☐	☐	☐
☐		☐	☐	☐	☐	☐	☐	☐	☐	☐	☐	☐	☐
☐		☐	☐	☐	☐	☐	☐	☐	☐	☐	☐	☐	☐

ALL NORTHEAST WILDLIFE SPECIES

The following is a list of all wildlife species (excluding invertebrates) whose current normal range includes at least part of the Northeast, which includes the following States: CT, RI, MA, VT, NH, and ME.

* indicates introduced species

BIRDS (321 SPECIES)

WATERFOWL
Snow Goose	Anser caerulescens
Greater White-Fronted Goose	Anser albifrons
Brant	Branta bernicla
Canada Goose	Branta canadensis
Mute Swan*	Cygnus olor
Wood Duck	Aix sponsa
Blue-Winged Teal	Spatula discors
Northern Shoveler	Spatula clypeata
Gadwall	Mareca strepera
Eurasian Wigeon	Mareca penelope
American Wigeon	Mareca americana
Mallard	Anas platyrhynchos
American Black Duck	Anas rubripes
Northern Pintail	Anas acuta
Green-Winged Teal	Anas crecca
Canvasback	Aythya valisineria
Redhead	Aythya americana
Ring-Necked Duck	Aythya collaris
Greater Scaup	Aythya marila
Lesser Scaup	Aythya affinis
King Eider	Somateria spectabilis
Common Eider	Somateria mollissima
Harlequin Duck	Histrionicus histrionicus
Surf Scoter	Melanitta perspicillata
White-Winged Scoter	Melanitta deglandi
Black Scoter	Melanitta americana
Long-Tailed Duck	Clangula hyemalis
Bufflehead	Bucephala albeola
Common Goldeneye	Bucephala clangula
Barrow's Goldeneye	Bucephala islandica
Hooded Merganser	Lophodytes cucullatus
Common Merganser	Mergus merganser
Red-Breasted Merganser	Mergus serrator
Ruddy Duck	Oxyura jamaicensis

GROUSE, QUAIL, AND ALLIES
Northern Bobwhite	Colinus virginianus
Wild Turkey	Meleagris gallopavo

GROUSE, QUAIL, AND ALLIES (CONTINUED)
Ruffed Grouse	Bonasa umbellus
Spruce Grouse	Canachites canadensis
Ring-Necked Pheasant*	Phasianus colchicus

GREBES
Pied-Billed Grebe	Podilymbus podiceps
Horned Grebe	Podiceps auratus
Red-Necked Grebe	Podiceps grisegena

PIGEONS AND DOVES
Rock Pigeon*	Columba livia
Mourning Dove	Zenaida macroura

CUCKOOS
Yellow-Billed Cuckoo	Coccyzus americanus
Black-Billed Cuckoo	Coccyzus erythropthalmus

NIGHTJARS
Common Nighthawk	Chordeiles minor
Chuck-Will's-widow	Antrostomus carolinensis
Eastern Whip-Poor-Will	Antrostomus vociferus

SWIFTS
Chimney Swift	Chaetura pelagica

HUMMINGBIRDS
Ruby-Throated Hummingbird	Archilochus colubris

RAILS, GALLINULES, AND ALLIES
King Rail	Rallus elegans
Clapper Rail	Rallus crepitans
Virginia Rail	Rallus limicola
Sora	Porzana carolina
Common Gallinule	Gallinula galeata
American Coot	Fulica americana

CRANES
Sandhill Crane	Antigone canadensis

Shorebirds

Common Name	Scientific Name
American Oystercatcher	*Haematopus palliatus*
Black-Bellied Plover	*Pluvialis squatarola*
American Golden-Plover	*Pluvialis dominica*
Killdeer	*Charadrius vociferus*
Semipalmated Plover	*Charadrius semipalmatus*
Piping Plover	*Charadrius melodus*
Upland Sandpiper	*Bartramia longicauda*
Whimbrel	*Numenius phaeopus*
Hudsonian Godwit	*Limosa haemastica*
Ruddy Turnstone	*Arenaria interpres*
Red Knot	*Calidris canutus*
Stilt Sandpiper	*Calidris himantopus*
Sanderling	*Calidris alba*
Dunlin	*Calidris alpina*
Purple Sandpiper	*Calidris maritima*
Least Sandpiper	*Calidris minutilla*
White-Rumped Sandpiper	*Calidris fuscicollis*
Buff-Breasted Sandpiper	*Calidris subruficollis*
Pectoral Sandpiper	*Calidris melanotos*
Semipalmated Sandpiper	*Calidris pusilla*
Short-Billed Dowitcher	*Limnodromus griseus*
Long-Billed Dowitcher	*Limnodromus scolopaceus*
American Woodcock	*Scolopax minor*
Wilson's Snipe	*Gallinago delicata*
Spotted Sandpiper	*Actitis macularius*
Solitary Sandpiper	*Tringa solitaria*
Lesser Yellowlegs	*Tringa flavipes*
Willet	*Tringa semipalmata*
Greater Yellowlegs	*Tringa melanoleuca*
Wilson's Phalarope	*Phalaropus tricolor*
Red-Necked Phalarope	*Phalaropus lobatus*
Red Phalarope	*Phalaropus fulicarius*

Skuas and Jaegers

Great Skua	*Stercorarius skua*
South Polar Skua	*Stercorarius maccormicki*
Pomarine Jaeger	*Stercorarius pomarinus*
Parasitic Jaeger	*Stercorarius parasiticus*
Long-Tailed Jaeger	*Stercorarius longicaudus*

Alcids

Dovekie	*Alle alle*
Common Murre	*Uria aalge*
Thick-Billed Murre	*Uria lomvia*
Razorbill	*Alca torda*
Black Guillemot	*Cepphus grille*
Atlantic Puffin	*Fratercula arctica*

Gulls, Terns, and Skimmers

Black-Legged Kittiwake	*Rissa tridactyla*
Bonaparte's Gull	*Chroicocephalus philadelphia*
Black-Headed Gull	*Chroicocephalus ridibundus*
Little Gull	*Hydrocoloeus minutus*
Laughing Gull	*Laucophaeus atricilla*
Ring-Billed Gull	*Larus delawarensis*
Herring Gull	*Larus argentatus*
Iceland Gull	*Larus glaucoides*
Lesser Black-Backed Gull	*Larus fuscus*
Glaucous Gull	*Larus hyperboreus*
Great Black-Backed Gull	*Larus marinus*
Least Tern	*Sternula antillarum*
Caspian Tern	*Hydroprogne caspia*
Black Tern	*Chlidonias niger*
Roseate Tern	*Sterna dougallii*
Common Tern	*Sterna hirundo*
Arctic Tern	*Sterna paradisaea*
Forster's Tern	*Sterna forsteri*
Royal Tern	*Thalasseus maximus*
Black Skimmer	*Rynchops niger*

Loons

Red-Throated Loon	*Gavia stellata*
Pacific Loon	*Gavia pacifica*
Common Loon	*Gavia immer*

Storm-Petrels

Wilson's Storm-Petrel	*Oceanites oceanicus*
Leach's Storm-Petrel	*Hydrobates leucorhous*

Petrels, Shearwaters, and Diving-Petrels

Northern Fulmar	*Fulmarus glacialis*
Cory's Shearwater	*Calonectris diomedea*
Sooty Shearwater	*Ardenna grisea*
Great Shearwater	*Ardenna gravis*
Manx Shearwater	*Puffinus puffinus*

Frigatebirds, Boobies, and Gannets

Common Name	Scientific Name
Northern Gannet	*Morus bassanus*

Cormorants and Anhingas

Common Name	Scientific Name
Great Cormorant	*Phalacrocorax carbo*
Double-Crested Cormorant	*Nannopterum auritum*

HERONS, IBIS, AND ALLIES

American Bittern — *Botaurus lentiginosus*
Least Bittern — *Ixobrychus exilis*
Great Blue Heron — *Ardea herodias*
Great Egret — *Ardea alba*
Snowy Egret — *Egretta thula*
Little Blue Heron — *Egretta caerulea*
Tricolored Heron — *Egretta tricolor*
Cattle Egret — *Bubulcus ibis*
Green Heron — *Butorides virescens*
Black-Crowned Night-Heron — *Nycticorax nycticorax*
Yellow-Crowned Night-Heron — *Nyctanassa violacea*
Glossy Ibis — *Plegadis falcinellus*

VULTURES, HAWKS, AND ALLIES

Black Vulture — *Coragyps atratus*
Turkey Vulture — *Cathartes aura*
Osprey — *Pandion haliaetus*
Mississippi Kite — *Ictinia mississippiensis*
Golden Eagle — *Aquila chrysaetos*
Northern Harrier — *Circus hudsonius*
Sharp-Shinned Hawk — *Accipiter striatus*
Cooper's Hawk — *Accipiter cooperii*
Northern Goshawk — *Accipiter gentilis*
Bald Eagle — *Haliaeetus leucocephalus*
Red-Shouldered Hawk — *Buteo lineatus*
Broad-Winged Hawk — *Buteo platypterus*
Red-Tailed Hawk — *Buteo jamaicensis*
Rough-Legged Hawk — *Buteo lagopus*

OWLS

Barn Owl — *Tyto alba*
Eastern Screech-Owl — *Megascops asio*
Great Horned Owl — *Bubo virginianus*
Snowy Owl — *Bubo scandiacus*
Barred Owl — *Strix varia*
Great Gray Owl — *Strix nebulosa*
Long-Eared Owl — *Asio otus*
Short-Eared Owl — *Asio flammeus*
Northern Saw-Whet Owl — *Aegolius acadicus*

KINGFISHERS

Belted Kingfisher — *Megaceryle alcyon*

WOODPECKERS

Yellow-Bellied Sapsucker — *Sphyrapicus varius*
Red-Headed Woodpecker — *Melanerpes erythrocephalus*

WOODPECKERS (CONTINUED)

Red-Bellied Woodpecker — *Melanerpes carolinus*
Black-Backed Woodpecker — *Picoides arcticus*
Downy Woodpecker — *Dryobates pubescens*
Hairy Woodpecker — *Dryobates villosus*
Northern Flicker — *Colaptes auratus*
Pileated Woodpecker — *Dryocopus pileatus*

FALCONS AND CARACARAS

American Kestrel — *Falco sparverius*
Merlin — *Falco columbarius*
Gyrfalcon — *Falco rusticolus*
Peregrine Falcon — *Falco peregrinus*

PARROTS, PARAKEETS, AND ALLIES

Monk Parakeet* — *Myiopsitta monachus*

TYRANT FLYCATCHERS: PEWEES, KINGBIRDS, AND ALLIES

Great Crested Flycatcher — *Myiarchus crinitus*
Eastern Kingbird — *Tyrannus tyrannus*
Olive-Sided Flycatcher — *Contopus cooperi*
Eastern Wood-Pewee — *Contopus virens*
Yellow-Bellied Flycatcher — *Empidonax flaviventris*
Acadian Flycatcher — *Empidonax virescens*
Alder Flycatcher — *Empidonax alnorum*
Willow Flycatcher — *Empidonax traillii*
Least Flycatcher — *Empidonax minimus*
Eastern Phoebe — *Sayornis phoebe*

VIREOS

White-Eyed Vireo — *Vireo griseus*
Yellow-Throated Vireo — *Vireo flavifrons*
Blue-Headed Vireo — *Vireo solitarius*
Philadelphia Vireo — *Vireo philadelphicus*
Warbling Vireo — *Vireo gilvus*
Red-Eyed Vireo — *Vireo olivaceus*

SHRIKES

Northern Shrike — *Lanius borealis*

JAYS, MAGPIES, CROWS, AND RAVENS

Blue Jay — *Cyanocitta cristata*
Canada Jay — *Perisoreus canadensis*
American Crow — *Corvus brachyrhynchos*
Fish Crow — *Corvus ossifragus*
Common Raven — *Corvus corax*

Tits, Chickadees, and Titmice
Black-Capped Chickadee — *Poecile atricapillus*
Boreal Chickadee — *Poecile hudsonicus*
Tufted Titmouse — *Baeolophus bicolor*

Larks
Horned Lark — *Eremophila alpestris*

Martins and Swallows
Bank Swallow — *Riparia riparia*
Tree Swallow — *Tachycineta bicolor*
Northern Rough-Winged Swallow — *Stelgidopteryx serripennis*
Purple Martin — *Progne subis*
Barn Swallow — *Hirundo rustica*
Cliff Swallow — *Petrochelidon pyrrhonota*

Kinglets
Ruby-Crowned Kinglet — *Corthylio calendula*
Golden-Crowned Kinglet — *Regulus satrapa*

Nuthatches
Red-Breasted Nuthatch — *Sitta canadensis*
White-Breasted Nuthatch — *Sitta carolinensis*

Treecreepers
Brown Creeper — *Certhia americana*

Gnatcatchers
Blue-Gray Gnatcatcher — *Polioptila caerulea*

Wrens
Carolina Wren — *Thryothorus ludovicianus*
House Wren — *Troglodytes aedon*
Winter Wren — *Troglodytes hiemalis*
Marsh Wren — *Cistothorus palustris*

Starlings and Mynas
European Starling* — *Sturnus vulgaris*

Catbirds, Mockingbirds, and Thrashers
Gray Catbird — *Dumetella carolinensis*
Brown Thrasher — *Toxostoma rufum*
Northern Mockingbird — *Mimus polyglottos*

Thrushes
Eastern Bluebird — *Sialia sialis*
Veery — *Catharus fuscescens*
Bicknell's Thrush — *Catharus bicknelli*

Thrushes (Continued)
Swainson's Thrush — *Catharus ustulatus*
Hermit Thrush — *Catharus guttatus*
Wood Thrush — *Hylocichla mustelina*
American Robin — *Turdus migratorius*

Waxwings
Bohemian Waxwing — *Bombycilla garrulus*
Cedar Waxwing — *Bombycilla cedrorum*

Old World Sparrows
House Sparrow* — *Passer domesticus*

Wagtails and Pipits
American Pipit — *Anthus rubescens*

Finches, Euphonias, and Allies
Evening Grosbeak — *Coccothraustes vespertinus*
Pine Grosbeak — *Pinicola enucleator*
House Finch* — *Haemorhous mexicanus*
Purple Finch — *Haemorhous purpureus*
Common Redpoll — *Acanthis flammea*
Hoary Redpoll — *Acanthis hornemanni*
Red Crossbill — *Loxia curvirostra*
White-Winged Crossbill — *Loxia leucoptera*
Pine Siskin — *Spinus pinus*
American Goldfinch — *Spinus tristis*

Longspurs and Snow Buntings
Lapland Longspur — *Calcarius lapponicus*
Snow Bunting — *Plectrophenax nivalis*

New World Sparrows
Grasshopper Sparrow — *Ammodramus savannarum*
Chipping Sparrow — *Spizella passerine*
Clay-Colored Sparrow — *Spizella pallida*
Field Sparrow — *Spizella pusilla*
Fox Sparrow — *Passerella iliaca*
American Tree Sparrow — *Spizelloides arborea*
Dark-Eyed Junco — *Junco hyemalis*
White-Crowned Sparrow — *Zonotrichia leucophrys*
White-Throated Sparrow — *Zonotrichia albicollis*
Vesper Sparrow — *Pooecetes gramineus*
Seaside Sparrow — *Ammospiza maritima*
Nelson's Sparrow — *Ammospiza nelson*
Saltmarsh Sparrow — *Ammospiza caudacuta*
Savannah Sparrow — *Passerculus sandwichensis*

New World Sparrows (Continued)

Song Sparrow	*Melospiza melodia*
Lincoln's Sparrow	*Melospiza lincolnii*
Swamp Sparrow	*Melospiza georgiana*
Eastern Towhee	*Pipilo erythrophthalmus*

Yellow-Breasted Chat

Yellow-Breasted Chat	*Icteria virens*

Blackbirds

Bobolink	*Dolichonyx oryzivorus*
Eastern Meadowlark	*Sturnella magna*
Orchard Oriole	*Icterus spurius*
Baltimore Oriole	*Icterus galbula*
Red-Winged Blackbird	*Agelaius phoeniceus*
Brown-Headed Cowbird	*Molothrus ater*
Rusty Blackbird	*Euphagus carolinus*
Common Grackle	*Quiscalus quiscula*

Wood-Warblers

Ovenbird	*Seiurus aurocapilla*
Worm-Eating Warbler	*Helmitheros vermivorum*
Louisiana Waterthrush	*Parkesia motacilla*
Northern Waterthrush	*Parkesia noveboracensis*
Golden-Winged Warbler	*Vermivora chrysoptera*
Blue-Winged Warbler	*Vermivora cyanoptera*
Black-and-White Warbler	*Mniotilta varia*
Prothonotary Warbler	*Protonotaria citrea*
Tennessee Warbler	*Leiothlypis peregrina*
Orange-Crowned Warbler	*Leiothlypis celata*
Nashville Warbler	*Leiothlypis ruficapilla*
Connecticut Warbler	*Oporornis agilis*
Mourning Warbler	*Geothlypis Philadelphia*
Kentucky Warbler	*Geothlypis Formosa*
Common Yellowthroat	*Geothlypis trichas*
Hooded Warbler	*Setophaga citrina*
American Redstart	*Setophaga ruticilla*
Cape May Warbler	*Setophaga tigrine*
Cerulean Warbler	*Setophaga cerulea*
Northern Parula	*Setophaga americana*
Magnolia Warbler	*Setophaga magnolia*
Bay-Breasted Warbler	*Setophaga castanea*
Blackburnian Warbler	*Setophaga fusca*
Yellow Warbler	*Setophaga petechia*
Chestnut-Sided Warbler	*Setophaga pensylvanica*
Blackpoll Warbler	*Setophaga striat*

Wood-Warblers (Continued)

Black-Throated Blue Warbler	*Setophaga caerulescens*
Palm Warbler	*Setophaga palmarum*
Pine Warbler	*Setophaga pinus*
Yellow-Rumped Warbler	*Setophaga coronate*
Yellow-Throated Warbler	*Setophaga dominica*
Prairie Warbler	*Setophaga discolor*
Black-Throated Green Warbler	*Setophaga virens*
Canada Warbler	*Cardellina canadensis*
Wilson's Warbler	*Cardellina pusilla*

Cardinals, Grosbeaks, and Allies

Summer Tanager	*Piranga rubra*
Scarlet Tanager	*Piranga olivacea*
Northern Cardinal	*Cardinalis cardinalis*
Rose-Breasted Grosbeak	*Pheucticus ludovicianus*
Blue Grosbeak	*Passerina caerulea*
Indigo Bunting	*Passerina cyanea*
Dickcissel	*Spiza americana*

MAMMALS (78 SPECIES)

Bears

American Black Bear	*Ursus americanus*

Canids (Dogs)

Eastern Coyote	*Canis latrans*
Gray Fox	*Urocyon cinereoargenteus*
Red Fox	*Vulpes vulpes*

Deer and Moose

White-Tailed Deer	*Odocoileus virginianus*
Moose	*Alces alces*

Felids (Cats)

Canada Lynx	*Lynx canadensis*
Bobcat	*Lynx rufus*

Beavers

American Beaver	*Castor canadensis*

Opossums

Virginia Opossum	*Didelphis virginiana*

Raccoons
Raccoon — *Procyon lotor*

Skunks
Striped Skunk — *Mephites mephites*

Porcupines
North American Porcupine — *Erethizon dorsatum*

Rabbits and Hares
Snowshore Hare — *Lepus americanus*
Eastern Cottontail* — *Sylvilagus floridanus*
New England Cottontail — *Sylvilagus transitionalis*

Weasels, Minks, Martens, Fishers, and Otters
River Otter — *Lontra canadensis*
American Marten — *Martes americana*
Ermine — *Mustela erminea*
Long-Tailed Weasel — *Mustela frenata*
American Mink — *Mustela vison*
Fisher — *Martes pennanti*

Squirrels, Chipmunks, and Marmots
Eastern Chipmunk — *Tamias striatus*
Woodchuck — *Marmota monax*
Eastern Gray Squirrel — *Sciurus carolinensis*
American Red Squirrel — *Tamiasciurus hudsonicus*
Northern Flying Squirrel — *Glaucomys sabrinus*
Southern Flying Squirrel — *Glaucomys volans*

Rats, Mice, Voles, Lemmings, and Muskrats
Black Rat* — *Rattus rattus*
White-Footed Mouse — *Peromyscus leucopus*
Deer Mouse — *Peromyscus maniculatus*
House Mouse* — *Mus musculus*
Southern Red-Backed Vole — *Clethrionomys gapperi*
Rock Vole — *Microtus chrotorrhinus*
Beach Vole — *Microtus breweri*
Meadow Vole — *Microtus pennsylvanicus*
Woodland Vole — *Microtus pinetorium*
Muskrat — *Ondatra zibethicus*
Eastern Gray Squirrel — *Sciurus carolinensis*
Northern Bog Lemming — *Synaptomys borealis*
Southern Bog Lemming — *Synaptomys cooperi*

Jumping Mice
Meadow Jumping Mouse — *Zapus hudsonius*
Woodland Jumping Mouse — *Napaeozapus insignis*

Shrews
Northern Short-Tailed Shrew — *Blarina brevicauda*
Least Shrew — *Cryptotis parva*
Masked Shrew — *Sorex cinereus*
Rock Shrew — *Sorex dispar*
Smoky Shrew — *Sorex fumeus*
Pygmy Shrew — *Microsorex hoyi*
American Water Shrew — *Sorex palustris*

Moles
Hairy-Tailed Mole — *Parascalops breweri*
Eastern Mole — *Scalopus aquaticus*
Star-Nosed Mole — *Condylura cristata*

Bats
Eastern Small-Footed Myotis — *Myotis leibii*
Little Brown Bat — *Myotis lucifugus*
Northern Long-Eared Bat — *Myotis septentrionalis*
Indiana Bat — *Myotis sodalis*
Silver-Haired Bat — *Lasionycteris noctivagans*
Tricolored Bat — *Perimyotis subflavus*
Big Brown Bat — *Eptesicus fuscus*
Red Bat — *Lasiurus borealis*
Hoary Bat — *Lasiurus cinereus*

Seals
Harbor Seal — *Phoca vitulina*
Gray Seal — *Halichoerus grypus*
Ringed Seal — *Pusa hispida*
Harp Seal — *Pagophilus groenlandicus*
Hooded Seal — *Cystophora cristata*

Right Whales
North Atlantic Right Whale — *Eubalaena glacialis*

Rorquals
Humpback Whale — *Megaptera novaeangliae*
Minke Whale — *Balaeonoptera acutorostrata*
Sei Whale — *Balaeonoptera borealis*
Fin Whale — *Balaeonoptera physalus*

Sperm Whales
Sperm Whale — *Physeter macrocephalus*

Dolphins
Atlantic White-Sided Dolphin — *Laucopleurus acutus*
Common Bottlenose Dolphin — *Tursiops truncatus*

Dolphins (Continued)
Short-Beaked Common Dolphin — *Delphinus delphis*
Killer Whale — *Orcinus orca*

Porpoises
Harbor Porpoise — *Phocoena phocoena*

AMPHIBIANS (24 species)

True Toads
American Toad — *Anaxyrus americanus*
Fowler's Toad — *Anaxyrus fowleri*

Tree Frogs
Gray Treefrog — *Hyla versicolor*
Spring Peeper — *Pseudacris crucifer*

True Frogs
American Bullfrog — *Lithobates catesbeianus*
Green Frog — *Lithobates clamitans*
Mink Frog — *Lithobates septentrionalis*
Wood Frog — *Lithobates sylvaticus*
Pickerel Frog — *Lithobates palustris*
Northern Leopard Frog — *Lithobates pipiens*
Mid-Atlantic Coast Leopard Frog — *Lithobates kauffeldi*

Spadefoots
Eastern Spadefoot — *Scaphiopus holbrookii*

Mole Salamanders
Jefferson Salamander — *Ambystoma jeffersonianum*
Blue-Spotted Salamander — *Ambystoma laterale*
Spotted Salamander — *Ambystoma maculatum*
Marbled Salamander — *Ambystoma opacum*

Lungless Salamanders
Four-Toed Salamander — *Hemidactylium scutatum*
Northern Dusky Salamander — *Desmognathus fuscus*
Spring Salamander — *Gyrinophilus porphyriticus*
Northern Two-Lined Salamander — *Eurycea bislineata*
Eastern Red-Backed Salamander — *Plethodon cinereus*
Northern Slimy Salamander — *Plethodon glutinosus*

Mudpuppies
Common Mudpuppy — *Necturus maculosus*

Newts
Eastern Newt — *Notophthalmus viridescens*

REPTILES (31 species)

Snapping Turtles
Snapping Turtle — *Chelydra serpentina*

Emydid Turtles
Blanding's Turtle — *Emydoidea blandingii*
Spotted Turtle — *Clemmys guttata*
Eastern Box Turtle — *Terrapene carolina*
Northern Red-Bellied Cooter — *Pseudemys rubriventris*
Painted Turtle — *Chysemys picta*
Wood Turtle — *Glyptemys insculpta*
Bog Turtle — *Glyptemys muhlenbergii*
Diamondback Terrapin — *Malaclemys terrapin*
Northern Map Turtle — *Graptemys geographica*

Mud and Musk Turtles
Eastern Musk Turtle — *Sternotherus odoratus*

Leatherback Sea Turtles
Leatherback — *Dermochelys coriacea*

Hard-Shelled Sea Turtles
Green Turtle — *Chelonia mydas*
Hawksbill — *Eretmochelys imbricata*
Loggerhead — *Caretta caretta*
Kemp's Ridley — *Chelonia mydas*

Skinks
Common Five-Lined Skink — *Plestidon fasciatus*

Pit Vipers
Eastern Copperhead — *Agkistrodon contortrix*
Timber Rattlesnake — *Crotalus horridus*

Colubrid Snakes
Eastern Wormsnake — *Carphophis amoenus*
Northern Black Racer — *Coluber constrictor*
Northern Ring-Necked Snake — *Diadophis punctatus*
Eastern Hog-Nosed Snake — *Heterodon platirhinos*
Eastern Milksnake — *Lampropeltis triangulum*
Common Watersnake — *Nerodia sipedon*
Smooth Greensnake — *Opheodrys vernalis*
Eastern Ratsnake — *Pantherophis alleghaniensis*
DeKay's Brownsnake — *Storeria dekayi*
Red-Bellied Snake — *Storeria occipitomaculata*
Eastern Ribbonsnake — *Thamnophis sauritus*
Common Gartersnake — *Thamnophis sirtalis*

Photographic Credits

The following are the citations for all photos present in this book. All unlisted here were from this book's author. Most were attained from Creative Commons licensing. They follow this citation format:
Page number. "*Photo title*" by *Photographer*. *Photo URL*. *License* *.
Modifications (optional).
* Index of unique license types is present at end of this section

Front Cover: "Red Fox" by Mark Faherty. Permission obtained by photographer.

Front Cover: "Spotted Salamander on Road" by Brett Thelen. Permission obtained by photographer.

Front Cover: "Cyanocitta-cristata-004" by Mdf. https://commons.wikimedia.org/wiki/File:Cyanocitta-cristata-004.jpg. CC By-SA 3.0.

Back Cover: "Wood Frogs Mating" by Nicole Freidenfelds. Permission obtained by photographer.

Back Cover: "About Author Photo" by Mary Howell. Permission obtained by photographer.

Page 1: "Eastern Box Turtle" by Lisabeth Willey. Permission obtained by photographer.

Page 4: "Baby Mallards (4459635443).jpg" by Kurt Bauschardt. https://www.flickr.com/photos/kurt-b/4459635443/. CC By-SA 2.0

Page 5: "Tree swallows at a nest box in JBWR (24844p).jpg" by Rhododendrites. https://commons.wikimedia.org/wiki/File:Tree_swallows_at_a_nest_box_in_JBWR_(24844p).jpg. CC By-SA 4.0 International.

Page 6: "Cooper's Hawk" by Mark Faherty. Permission obtained by photographer.

Page 7 (line drawing): "Flickers (PSF)" by Pearson Scott Foresman. https://commons.wikimedia.org/wiki/File:Flickers_(PSF).png. Public Domain licensed.

Page 8: "belted kingfisher, shell creek" by Russ. https://flickr.com/photos/81751903@N08/31924578986. CC By 2.0. Cropped.

Page 9: "Great Blue Heron" by Tony Alter. https://www.flickr.com/photos/78428166@N00/8708141027. CC By 2.0. Cropped.

Page 10: "Great egret (Ardea alba) with green facial skin" by Rotareneg. https://commons.wikimedia.org/wiki/File:Great_egret_(Ardea_alba)_with_green_facial_skin.jpg. CC By-SA 4.0.

Photographic Credits

Page 11: "Gavia Immer CommonLoon LkCoochiching.jpg" by Mykola Swarnyk. https://commons.wikimedia.org/wiki/File:Gavia_Immer_CommonLoon_LkCoochiching.jpg. CC By-SA 3.0. Cropped.

Page 12: "Double-crested cormorant at Sutro Baths-6942" by Frank Schulenburg. https://en.m.wikipedia.org/wiki/File:Double-crested_cormorant_at_Sutro_Baths-6942.jpg. CC By-SA 4.0.

Page 13: "Canada Goose -Branta canadensis" by The High Fin Sperm Whale. https://commons.wikimedia.org/wiki/File:Canada_Goose_-Branta_canadensis.JPG. CC By-SA 3.0.

Page 14: "Cygnus olor (Küken) - Arboretum 2011-06-01 14-40-18.JPG" by Roland zh. https://commons.wikimedia.org/wiki/File:Cygnus_olor_(K%C3%BCken)_-_Arboretum_2011-06-01_14-40-18.JPG. CC By-SA 3.0.

Page 15: "1-IMG_8448aa" by Nigel. https://www.flickr.com/photos/winnu/15510279905. CC By-2.0. Cropped.

Page 16: "Moscow, Russia, Ducks" by Vyacheslav Argenberg. https://commons.wikimedia.org/wiki/File:Moscow,_Russia,_Ducks.jpg. CC By-SA 4.0 International. Cropped.

Page 17: "Storskrake / Common Merganser" by Asa Berndtsson. https://flickr.com/photos/93892629@N07/20351118125. CC By 2.0. Cropped.

Page 18: "Lophodytes cucullatus m Humber Bay" by Mykola Swarnyk. https://commons.wikimedia.org/wiki/File:Lophodytes_cucullatus_m_Humber_Bay.jpg. CC By-SA 3.0. Cropped.

Page 19: "Herring Gull (Larus argentatus)" by Christine Matthews. https://www.geograph.org.uk/photo/2923835. CC-By-SA 2.0.

Page 20: "Ring-billed gull (Larus delawarensis)" by Mark Nenadov. https://flickr.com/photos/34157166@N08/33299083036. CC By 2.0.

Page 21: "Turkey Vulture Cathartes aura" by gailhampshire. https://www.flickr.com/photos/gails_pictures/26122773156. CC By 2.0. Cropped.

Page 22: "Osprey, 2023-09-28.jpg" by Bnuuy. https://commons.wikimedia.org/wiki/File:Osprey,_2023-09-28.jpg. Public Domain licensed. Cropped.

Page 23: "Bald-eagle-160.jpg" by William H. Majoros. https://commons.wikimedia.org/wiki/File:Bald-eagle-160.jpg. CC By-SA 3.0. Cropped.

Page 24: "Red-Tailed Hawk" by CheepShot. https://www.flickr.com/photos/23755697@N04/7849220782. CC By 2.0.

Photographic Credits

Page 25: "Cooper's hawk in Prospect Park (22513)" by Rhododendrites. https://commons.wikimedia.org/wiki/File:Cooper%27s_hawk_in_Prospect_Park_(22513).jpg. CC By-SA 4.0 International.

Page 26: "Falco peregrinus f Humber Bay Park Toronto" by Mykola Swarnyk. https://commons.wikimedia.org/wiki/File:Falco_peregrinus_f_Humber_Bay_Park_Toronto.jpg. CC By-SA 3.0.

Page 27: "AmericanKestrel02" by Greg Hume. https://commons.wikimedia.org/wiki/File:AmericanKestrel02.jpg. CC By-SA 3.0.

Page 28: "Great horned owl (46526)" by Rhododendrites. https://commons.wikimedia.org/wiki/File:Great_horned_owl_(46526).jpg. CC By-SA 4.0 International.

Page 29: "Barred Owl - Strix varia, Wes Skiles Peacock Springs State Park, Luraville, Florida" by Judy Gallagher. https://www.flickr.com/photos/52450054@N04/6980706074. CC By 2.0.

Page 30: "Ruby-throated hummingbird" by Matt Tillett. https://www.flickr.com/photos/39955531@N00/5759988614. CC By 2.0. Cropped.

Page 31: "Downy Woodpecker-Male" by Ken Thomas. https://commons.wikimedia.org/wiki/File:Downy_Woodpecker-Male.jpg. Public Domain licensed.

Page 32: "Northern Flicker-27527" by Ken Thomas. https://commons.wikimedia.org/wiki/File:Northern_Flicker-27527.jpg. Public Domain licensed.

Page 33: "White Breasted Nuthatch" by Jocelyn Anderson. https://commons.wikimedia.org/wiki/File:White_Breasted_Nuthatch_(163824683).jpeg. CC By 3.0.

Page 34: "Blue Jay" by Jongsun Lee. https://commons.wikimedia.org/wiki/File:Blue_Jay_(210140531).jpeg. CC By 3.0.

Page 35: "Cardinalis cardinalis –Columbus, Ohio, USA-male-8 (1)" by Stephen Wolfe. https://commons.wikimedia.org/wiki/File:Cardinalis_cardinalis_-Columbus,_Ohio,_USA-male-8_(1).jpg. CC By 2.0.

Page 36: "American Robin 2006" by Mgiganteus. https://commons.wikimedia.org/wiki/File:American_Robin_2006.jpg. CC By-SA 2.5.

Page 37: "Icterus galbula PP.jpg" by Cephas. https://commons.wikimedia.org/wiki/File:Icterus_galbula_PP.jpg. CC By-SA 3.0. Cropped.

PHOTOGRAPHIC CREDITS

Page 38: "Sialia sialis -Michigan, USA -pair-8b" by Sandysphotos2009. https://commons.wikimedia.org/wiki/File:Sialia_sialis_-Michigan,_USA_-pair-8b.jpg. CC By 2.0.

Page 39: "Mourning Dove 2006" by Alan D. Wilson. https://commons.wikimedia.org/wiki/File:Mourning_Dove_2006.jpg. CC By-SA 2.5.

Page 40: "Catbird, Lebanon State Forest N.J." by Peter Massas. https://commons.wikimedia.org/wiki/File:Dumetella_carolinensis_-Brendan_T._Byrne_State_Forest,_New_Jersey,_USA-8.jpg. CC By-SA 2.0.

Page 41: "Charlie MockingBird Parker Backyard Birds Cary NC 0817" by bobistraveling. https://www.flickr.com/photos/bobistraveling/5446906354. CC By 2.0. Cropped.

Page 42: "Sturnus vulgaris Paris.jpg" by Jean-Jacques Boujot. https://commons.wikimedia.org/wiki/File:Sturnus_vulgaris_Paris.jpg. CC By-SA 2.0.

Page 43: "Common Grackle [33/100]" by Tim Sackton. https://flickr.com/photos/43581314@N08/33973682813. CC By-SA 2.0.

Page 44: "Corvus brachyrhynchos 1 (1).jpg" by Jack Wolf. https://commons.wikimedia.org/wiki/File:Corvus_brachyrhynchos_1_(1).jpg. CC By 2.0.

Page 45: "Eastern phoebe (01972).jpg" by Rhododendrites. https://commons.wikimedia.org/wiki/File:Eastern_phoebe_(01972).jpg. CC By-SA 4.0 International. Cropped.

Page 46: "Cedar Waxwing - Bombycilla cedrorum, George Washington's Birthplace National Monument, Colonial Beach, Virginia" by Judy Gallagher. https://flickr.com/photos/52450054@N04/39997434862. CC By 2.0.

Page 47: "Tufted Titmouse" by Andy Reago and Chrissy McClarren. https://www.flickr.com/photos/wildreturn/24611352525/. CC By 2.0. Cropped.

Page 48: "Black-capped Chickadee (Poecile atricapillus) - Cambridge, Ontario 01.jpg" by Ryan Hodnett. https://commons.wikimedia.org/wiki/File:Black-capped_Chickadee_(Poecile_atricapillus)_-_Cambridge,_Ontario_01.jpg. CC By-SA 4.0 International.

Page 49: "American goldfinch in PP (12544)" by Rhododendrites. https://commons.wikimedia.org/wiki/File:American_goldfinch_in_PP_(12544).jpg. CC By-SA 4.0 International.

Page 50: "What's the difference between…" by Dawn Huczek. https://www.flickr.com/photos/31064702@N05/3696885271. CC By 2.0. Cropped.

Photographic Credits

Page 51: "Song sparrow (MA)" by Bill Thompson. https://www.flickr.com/photos/usfwsnortheast/6322873441. Public Domain photo. Cropped.

Page 52: "House Sparrow (m), Breeding Plumage" by Becky Matsubara. https://www.flickr.com/photos/beckymatsubara/27424329288. CC By 2.0. Cropped.

Page 53: "Carolina Wrens feeding invisible young in a nest under the Tree base" by Andy Reago and Chrissy McClarren. https://www.flickr.com/photos/80270393@N06/50345786272. CC By 2.0. Cropped.

Page 54: "Meleagris gallopavo displaying at Deer Island Open Space Preserve.jpg" by Frank Schulenberg. https://commons.wikimedia.org/wiki/File:Meleagris_gallopavo_displaying_at_Deer_Island_Open_Space_Preserve.jpg. CC By-SA 4.0 International.

Page 55: "Pileated Woodpecker (Dryocopus pileatus)" by Dominic Sherony. https://commons.wikimedia.org/wiki/File:Dryocopus_pileatus_01.jpg. CC By 2.0. Cropped.

Page 56: "Male cowbird" by Jmalik at English Wikipedia. https://commons.wikimedia.org/wiki/File:Malecowbird.jpg. CC By-SA 3.0.

Page 57: "red-winged blackbird neighborhood 6.11.20 DSC_7982" by Laura Wolf. https://flickr.com/photos/151817352@N04/50051801922. CC By 2.0. Cropped.

Page 58: "Wood Thrush" by CheepShot. https://www.flickr.com/photos/23755697@N04/8722948663. CC By 2.0.

Page 59: "Ovenbird93" by S. Maslowski, USFWS. https://upload.wikimedia.org/wikipedia/commons/9/92/Ovenbird93.jpg. Public Domain licensed. Cropped.

Page 60: "Eastern Kingbird" by Don Faulkner. https://flickr.com/photos/50763319@N04/14683057984. CC By-SA 2.0.

Page 61: "Tree swallow at Stroud Preserve" by Iiii I I I. https://commons.wikimedia.org/wiki/File:Tree_swallow_at_Stroud_Preserve.jpg. CC By-SA 4.0.

Page 62: "DSC_0066" by 測鏡者. https://flickr.com/photos/63178782@N04/32629342832. CC By-SA 2.0. Cropped.

Page 63 (line drawing): "Raccoon (PSF)" by Pearson Scott Foresman. https://commons.wikimedia.org/wiki/File:Racoon_(PSF).png. Public Domain licensed.

Page 64: "Ursus americanus PO 03" by Simon Pierre Barrette. https://commons.wikimedia.org/wiki/File:Ursus_americanus_PO_03.jpg. CC By-SA 3.0.

PHOTOGRAPHIC CREDITS

Page 65: "Bull Moose" by Larry Lamsa.
https://www.flickr.com/photos/larry1732/51509212853. CC By 3.0. Cropped.

Page 66: "White-tailed deer" by Scott Bauer, USDA.
https://www.ars.usda.gov/oc/images/photos/may01/k5437-3. Public Domain licensed.

Page 67: "Coyote-face-tail-snow-mouth - West Virginia - ForestWander.jpg" by https://www.forestwander.com.
https://commons.wikimedia.org/wiki/File:Coyote-face-tail-snow-mouth_-_West_Virginia_-_ForestWander.jpg. CC By-SA 3.0.

Page 68: "Bobcat2" by Calibas.
https://commons.wikimedia.org/wiki/File:Bobcat2.jpg. Public Domain licensed.

Page 69: "Photo 6568101" by Joanne Redwood.
https://web.archive.org/web/20191109175140/https://www.inaturalist.org/photos/6568101. Public Domain licensed. Cropped.

Page 70: "Gray Fox" by Tammy Mealman, USFWS.
https://commons.wikimedia.org/wiki/File:Gray_Fox_(35870741011).jpg. Public Domain licensed. Cropped.

Page 71: "Castor canadensis - Wilhelma Zoo - Stuttgard, Germany - DSC02125" by Daderot.
https://commons.wikimedia.org/wiki/File:Castor_canadensis_-_Wilhelma_Zoo_-_Stuttgart,_Germany_-_DSC02125.jpg. CC0 1.0.

Page 72: "River otter dive sequence (1)" by Josh Spice, USNPS.
https://www.flickr.com/photos/yellowstonenps/49705455553. Public Domain licensed. Cropped.

Page 73: "Porcupine" by Courtney Celley, USFWS.
https://www.flickr.com/photos/usfwsmidwest/5670622729. Public Domain licensed.

Page 74: "Fishers" by Emily Brouwer, USNPS.
https://flickr.com/photos/78037339@N03/14584727897. CC By 2.0.

Page 75: "DSC_2721" by Keith and Kasia Moore.
https://www.flickr.com/photos/30633905@N03/4838604886. CC By-SA 2.0. Cropped.

Page 76: "Marmota monax UL 10" by Cephas.
https://commons.wikimedia.org/wiki/File:Marmota_monax_UL_10.jpg. CC By-SA 4.0 International.

Page 77: "California Raccoon" by Fazalmajid.
https://en.m.wikipedia.org/wiki/File:California_Raccoon.jpg. CC By-SA 3.0.

Photographic Credits

Page 78: "Didelphis virginiana with young" by Specialjake. https://commons.wikimedia.org/wiki/File:Didelphis_virginiana_with_young.JPG. CC By-SA 3.0.

Page 79: "Striped Skunk (Mephitis mephitis) DSC_0030" by Dan Dzurisin. https:///www.flickr.com/photos/8987884@N07/4548287441. CC By 2.0.

Page 80: "Eastern Cottontail (Sylvilagus floridanus)" by The High Fin Sperm Whale. https://commons.wikimedia.org/wiki/File:Eastern_Cottontail_(Sylvilagus_floridanus).JPG. CC By-SA 3.0.

Page 81: "Little Brown Myotis" by SMBishop. https://commons.wikimedia.org/wiki/File:Little_Brown_Myotis.JPG. CC By-SA 3.0.

Page 82: "Eastern Grey Squirrel in Bunhill Fields" by HH58. https://commons.wikimedia.org/wiki/File:Eastern_Grey_Squirrel_in_Bunhill_Fields.jpg. CC By-SA 4.0 International.

Page 83: "Tamiasciurus hudsonicus CT 08" by Cephas. https://commons.wikimedia.org/wiki/File:Tamiasciurus_hudsonicus_CT_08.jpg. CC By 4.0 International.

Page 84: "Southern Flying Squirrel - Glaucomys volans, Arlington, Virginia, December 22, 2020" by Judy Gallagher. https://www.flickr.com/photos/52450054@N04/53406816432. CC By 2.0. Rotated.

Page 85: "Photo 162560197" by Alexis Godin. https://www.inaturalist.org/photos/162560197. CC By 4.0 International.

Page 86: "Ondatra zibethicus CT 02" by Simon Pierre Barrette. https://commons.wikimedia.org/wiki/File:Ondatra_zibethicus_CT_02.jpg. CC By-SA 4.0 International.

Page 87: "Condylura" by USNPS. https://commons.wikimedia.org/wiki/File:Condylura.jpg. Public Domain licensed.

Page 88: "Baby meadow vole" by Chuck Homler. https://commons.wikimedia.org/wiki/File:Baby_meadow_vole.jpg. CC By 3.0.

Page 89 (line drawing): "Wood Frog-TSF 0040" by Bradlee Whidden. https://commons.wikimedia.org/wiki/File:Wood_Frog-TSF_0040.jpg. Public Domain licensed.

Page 90: "Photo 217228914" by Zygy. https://www.inaturalist.org/photos/217228914. CC0 1.0.

Page 91: "North-American-bullfrog1" by Carl D. Howe. https://commons.wikimedia.org/wiki/File:North-American-bullfrog1.jpg. CC By-SA 2.5.

Photographic Credits

Page 92: "Spring Peeper Calling" by Justin Meissen. https://www.flickr.com/photos/40855483@N00/13170934764. CC By-SA 2.0. Cropped.

Page 93: "Gray treefrog amplexus" by Fredlyfish4. https://commons.wikimedia.org/wiki/File:Gray_treefrog_amplexus.JPG. CC By-SA 3.0.

Page 94: "Eastern American Toad (Anaxyrus americanus americanus) - London, Ontario 01.jpg" by Ryan Hodnett. https://commons.wikimedia.org/wiki/File:Eastern_American_Toad_(Anaxyrus_americanus_americanus)_-_London,_Ontario_01.jpg. CC By-SA 4.0 International.

Page 95: "Eastern Spadefoot Amplexus" by Brad Timm.

Page 96: "Ambystoma maculatum" by Jared C. Benedict. https://commons.wikimedia.org/wiki/File:Ambystoma_maculatum.jpg. CC By-SA 3.0.

Page 97: "Adult Female Plethodon cinereus" by Alex Karasoulos. https://commons.wikimedia.org/wiki/File:Adult_Female_Plethodon_cinereus.jpg. CC By-SA 4.0 International.

Page 98: "Northern Two-lined Salamander" by Katja Schulz. https://flickr.com/photos/86548370@N00/29675570776. CC By 2.0.

Page 99: "Eastern newt red eft stage Sep 3 2012 North Fork Mountain near Chimney Top" by Jason Quinn. https://commons.wikimedia.org/wiki/File:Eastern_newt_red_eft_stage_Sep_3_2012_North_Fork_Mountain_near_Chimney_Top.jpg. CC By-SA 3.0.

Page 100 (line drawing): "Spotted Turtle-TSF 0014" by Bradlee Whidden. https://commons.wikimedia.org/wiki/File:Spotted_Turtle-TSF_0014.jpg. Public Domain licensed.

Page 101: "Eastern Box Turtle" by Jim Lynch, USNPS. https://www.flickr.com/photos/npsncbn/14979452692. CC By-SA 2.0.

Page 102: "Eastern Painted Turtle" by Danielle Brigida. https://www.flickr.com/photos/brigida/49866261538. CC By 2.0. Cropped.

Page 103: "Clemmys_guttata_SERC_04-07-11" by Smithsonian Environmental Research Center. https://flickr.com/photos/117184384@N07/12750541464. CC By 2.0.

Page 104: "Common Snapping Turtle 1429" by Mjbaker. https://commons.wikimedia.org/wiki/File:Common_Snapping_Turtle_1429.jpg. CC By 2.5.

Page 105: "Wood Turtle" by Trisha Shears. https://commons.wikimedia.org/wiki/File:WoodTurtle.jpg. Public Domain licensed.

PHOTOGRAPHIC CREDITS

Page 106: "Garter Snake" by Blaine Hansel.
https://commons.wikimedia.org/wiki/File:Garter_Snake.jpg. CC By 2.0.

Page 107: "Diadophis punctatus edwardsii4" by Cody Hough.
https://commons.wikimedia.org/wiki/File:Diadophis_punctatus_edwardsii4.jpg. CC By-SA 3.0.

Page 108: "Kingsnake" by Trista Rada.
https://www.flickr.com/photos/32916828@N06/3071284676. CC By 2.0.

Page 109: "Iowaherps-heterodon platirhinos" by Don F. Becker.
https://commons.wikimedia.org/wiki/File:Iowaherps-heterodon_platirhinos.jpg. CC By-SA 4.0.

Page 110: "Nerodia sipedon Stanton 3"by Riley Stanton.
https://commons.wikimedia.org/wiki/File:Nerodia_sipedon_Stanton_3.jpg. CC By-SA 4.0 International.

Page 115: "Moths galore!" by Ben Sale.
https://www.flickr.com/photos/33398884@N03/14726831142. CC By 2.0. Cropped.

Page 117: "American Toad on Road" by Brett Thelen. Permission obtained by photographer.

Page 118: "Do_not_feed_our_ducks_-_geograph.org.uk_-_942538" by Evelyn Simak. https://www.geograph.org.uk/photo/942538. CC By-SA 2.0.

Page 119: "Chuck and Liz_IMG_2079.jpg" by USNPS.
https://npgallery.nps.gov/AssetDetail/b64895a5-8452-4b83-b1e0-e8dc6a3f65e2. Public Domain licensed. Cropped.

PHOTOGRAPHIC CREDITS

Below are the locations for all Creative Commons licenses present in the preceding pages. They follow this format:
License name. License URL.

CC0 1.0. https://creativecommons.org/publicdomain/zero/1.0/.

CC By 2.0. https://creativecommons.org/licenses/by/2.0/.

CC-By-SA 2.0. https://creativecommons.org/licenses/by-sa/2.0/.

CC By-SA 2.5. https://creativecommons.org/licenses/by-sa/2.5/.

CC By 3.0. https://creativecommons.org/licenses/by/3.0/.

CC By-SA 3.0. https://creativecommons.org/licenses/by-sa/3.0/.

CC By-SA 4.0. https://creativecommons.org/licenses/by-sa/4.0/.

CC By 4.0 International. https://creativecommons.org/licenses/by/4.0/.

CC By-SA 4.0 International. https://creativecommons.org/licenses/by-sa/4.0/.

Public Domain licensed. https://en.wikipedia.org/wiki/Public_domain.

INDEX

American Black Bear **64**, 85, 115, 116
American Bullfrog **91**
American Crow 25, 34, **44**, 95
American Goldfinch **49**
American Kestrel **27**
American Red Squirrel **83**, 84
American Robin **36**, 43
American Toad **94**
anti-freeze 90, 92
anting 32, 41
Bald Eagle **23**
Baltimore Oriole **37**
Barred Owl **29**
Beaver 18, 38, 60, 61, **71**, 72, 73, 86, 103, 110
Belted Kingfisher **8**
birdhouse 52, 84, 93, 120
Black-Capped Chickadee 47, **48**
Blue Jay **34**
Bobcat **68**
broken-wing display 39, 59
Brown-Headed Cowbird 40, 49, **56**, 58, 60
burrow 8, 67, 71, 72, 75, 76, 79, 85, 86, 88, 95, 96, 101, 109, 110
cache 31, 33, 32, 34, 47, 69, 82
Canada Goose **13**
Carolina Wren 47, **53**
cavity-nesting 7, 8, 15, 31, 33, 38, 42, 55
Cedar Waxwing **46**
colony-nesting 9, 10, 12, 19, 43
Common Gartersnake **106**
Common Grackle **43**
Common Loon **11**
Common Merganser **17**, 18

Common Watersnake **110**
Cooper's Hawk **25**, 27
courtship behavior 18, 19, 20, 24, 28, 30, 97, 98
DDT 22, 23, 26
den 64, 67, 68, 69, 70, 72, 73, 75, 77, 79, 82, 106
Double-Crested Cormorant **12**
Downy Woodpecker **31**
Eastern Bluebird **38**, 42
Eastern Box Turtle **101**
Eastern Chipmunk 75, **85**
Eastern Cottontail 75, **80**
Eastern Coyote **66**, 70
Eastern Gray Squirrel **82**, 83, 84
Eastern Hognose Snake **109**
Eastern Kingbird **60**
Eastern Milksnake **108**
Eastern Newt **99**
Eastern Phoebe **45**
Eastern Red-Backed Salamander **97**, 98, 107
Eastern Spadefoot **95**
egg incubation 16, 24, 31, 50, 61, 62
egg-dumping 15, 17, 18
European Starling 38, **42**, 43
Fisher **74**, 76
Fox
    Gray **70**
    Red **69**, 70
Gray Catbird **40**, 121
Gray Fox **70**
Gray Treefrog 92, **93**
Great Blue Heron **9**

155

INDEX

Great Blue Heron **9**
Great Egret **10**
Great Horned Owl **28**, 29
Gull
   Herring **19**
   Ring-Billed **20**
Hawk
   Cooper's **25**, 27
   Red-Tailed 23, **24**
Herring Gull **19**
hibernation 76, 79, 81, 85, 106, 113
Hooded Merganser **18**
House Finch **50**
House Sparrow 38, **52**
hunting by humans 15, 18, 66, 72
introduced species 14, 38, 42, 46, 50, 52, 62, 80, 91, 102
Little Brown Bat **81**
Long-Tailed Weasel **75**
Mallard **16**, 90
mange 70
mate fidelity 13, 14, 19, 23, 24, 25, 26, 33, 36, 42, 53, 54, 57, 58, 62, 69, 70, 82
Meadow Vole **88**
Merganser
   Common **17**, 18
   Hooded **18**
Migratory Bird Treaty Act 10, 20
mimic 27, 34, 39, 40, 41, 42, 121
Moose **65**
Mourning Dove **39**, 62
Muskrat 77, **86**
Mute Swan **14**

nest box 15, 27, 38, 61
North American Porcupine **73**
North American River Otter **72**
Northern Cardinal **35**, 47
Northern Flicker **32**, 43
Northern Mockingbird 40, **41**, 121
Northern Ring-Necked Snake **107**
Northern Two-Lined Salamander **98**
Osprey **22**, 23, 26
Ovenbird 59
overwintering 21, 39, 40, 45, 57, 60, 81, 91, 98, 102, 104, 105, 108, 110, 113, 114
Owl
   Barred **29**
   Great-Horned **28**, 29
Painted Turtle **102**
Peregrine Falcon **26**, 27
Pileated Woodpecker **55**
prey constriction 108
rabies 77, 78
Raccoon 55, 67, **77**, 115
Red Fox **69**, 70
Red-Tailed Hawk 23, **24**
Red-Winged Blackbird 43, **57**
Ring-Billed Gull **20**
Rock Pigeon 26, **62**
roosting 9, 21, 29, 36, 44, 53, 54, 55, 57, 81
Ruby-Throated Hummingbird **30**
Salamander
   Eastern Red-Backed **97**, 98, 107
   Northern Two-Lined **98**
   Spotted **96**

Index

Snake
    Common Gartersnake **106**
    Common Watersnake **110**
    Eastern Hognose **109**
    Eastern Milksnake **108**
    Northern Ring-Necked **107**
Snapping Turtle **104**
Song Sparrow **51**
Southern Flying Squirrel 55, **84**
Sparrow
    House 38, **52**
    Song **51**
Spotted Salamander **96**
Spotted Turtle **103**
Spring Peeper **92**, 93
Squirrel
    American Red **83**, 84
    Eastern Gray **82**, 83, 84
    Southern Flying 55, **84**
Star-Nosed Mole **87**
Striped Skunk 67, 68, 69, **79**, 115
Tree Swallow **61**
Tufted Titmouse **47**
Turkey Vulture **21**
Turtle
    Eastern Box **101**
    Painted **102**
    Snapping **104**
    Spotted **103**
    Wood **105**
Virginia Opossum 47, 68, **78**
White-Breasted Nuthatch 31, **33**
White-Tailed Deer **66**

Wild Turkey **54**
Woodchuck 47, 69, **76**
Wood Duck **15**, 17, 18
Wood Frog **90**, 92, 93
Wood Thrush **58**
Wood Turtle **105**

Notes

This section is included as a space for you to jot down any notes related to wildlife encounters you have, nature outings you take, etc.

Notes

Notes

www.ingramcontent.com/pod-product-compliance
Lightning Source LLC
Chambersburg PA
CBHW052031030426
42337CB00027B/4947